Scholastic World Cultures

CHINA

by Daniel Chu

Third Edition

Consultant

CHESTER C. TAN, Ph.D.

Professor of History,
New York University.

Readability Consultant

LAWRENCE B. CHARRY, Ed.D.

 SCHOLASTIC INC.

Titles in This Series
CANADA
CHINA
GREAT BRITAIN
THE INDIAN SUBCONTINENT
JAPAN
LATIN AMERICA
MEXICO
THE MIDDLE EAST
SOUTHEAST ASIA
THE SOVIET UNION AND EASTERN EUROPE
TROPICAL AND SOUTHERN AFRICA

ISBN No. 0-590-34605-9

Daniel Chu is an associate editor with Time, Inc. Born in China, he came to the U.S. during World War II. A former associate editor of Scholastic Magazines, he is the coauthor of *A Glorious Age in Africa: The Story of Three Great African Empires* and *Passage to the Golden Gate: A History of the Chinese in America.*

General Editor for WORLD CULTURES: Carolyn Jackson
Special Editor: Lee Christenson
Assistant Editor: Elise Bauman
Teaching Guide Editor: Frances Plotkin

Art Director and Designer: Irmgard Lochner
Photo Editors: Elnora Bode, Linda Sykes

COVER: Chinese students of all ages turn out to greet American visitors in the city of Wuhan.

CHINA

Table of Contents

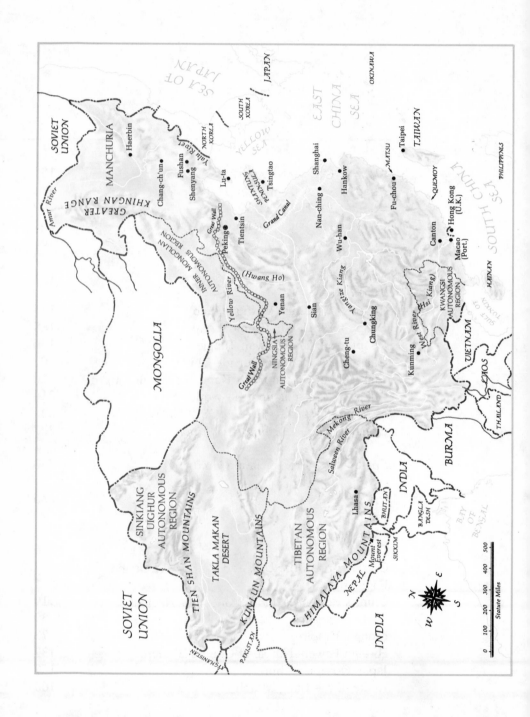

There are those who say we should not open our windows, because open windows let in flies and other insects. They want the windows to stay closed, so we all expire from lack of air. But we say, "Open the windows, breathe the fresh air, and at the same time, fight the flies and insects."

TENG HSIAO-PING

PROLOGUE

THAT PLACE
CALLED CHINA

ON MARCH 1, 1979, the American flag was hoisted over the new U.S. embassy in Peking. The fluttering Stars and Stripes marked the official end of a 30-year break between the U.S. and the People's Republic of China. From cola drinks to jumbo jets, trade between the two countries was now booming. Tens of thousands of American tourists were flocking to China every year.

The 1970's brought a turnabout in U.S.- Chinese relations. Ten years before, the two countries were not on speaking terms. Most Americans knew very little about China. Most Chinese knew even less about America. Even today with all the new contacts, an air of mystery remains. The dramatic changes of the 1970's and the 1980's have given us a more detailed picture of China. But it is still incomplete.

Suppose you were to ask the next four persons you meet to tell you, in a single short phrase, what each of them knows about China or the Chinese. Chances are pretty good that you would wind up with a series of statements that might go something like this:

China is a big, crowded place.

Almost everybody in China is poor.

The Chinese eat rice.

The Chinese do most things backward.

These are some of the more commonly held images of China and its people. But are these statements true? Well, yes — as far as they go.

Anyone who wants a more meaningful understanding of what China is all about, however, soon discovers that China is too big and too varied to be summed up with a series of one-liners. To illustrate, let's take a closer look at the four statements above:

A crowded China. Population experts agree that China is the world's most populous country — that is, it has more people living within its borders than any other single country in the world. But no one really knows, in fact, just how many people there are in China today.

Various estimates now place China's population at somewhere around one billion people. And even these guesses may be off by quite a few million, either too high or too low.

A poverty-stricken land. China is a "have not" na-

COMPARISON OF THE U. S. AND CHINA IN AREA AND POPULATION

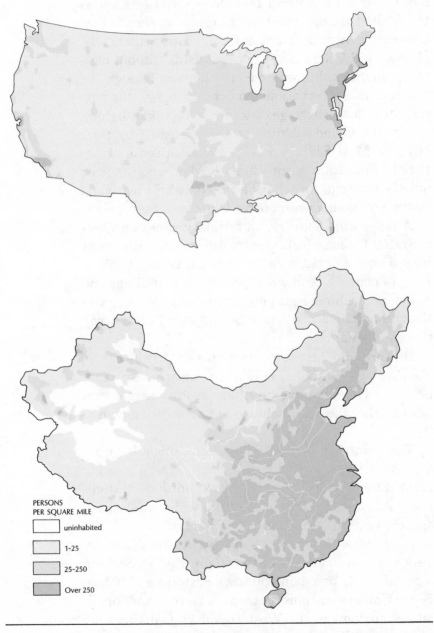

PERSONS PER SQUARE MILE

	uninhabited
	1-25
	25-250
	Over 250

Is China a crowded country? How does it compare with the U.S.? Where do most Chinese live?

tion. Incomes and living standards are lower than those in more advanced industrial societies such as the United States, Western Europe, or Japan. Few Chinese enjoy such things as family cars, private telephones, or TV sets. Some areas are still without electricity and running water in the homes. Though the threat of mass starvation is much less today, the possibility of food shortages can never be taken lightly.

Yet the Chinese have not been crushed by their poverty. Most Chinese have an intense sense of national pride. Rare is the Chinese who is not at least quietly thankful for what he thinks is his great good fortune of having been born a Chinese.

A rice-eating country. In ordinary times an average adult Chinese feels hungry unless he consumes at least a pound of rice a day (along with other kinds of food, of course). And when you think of millions and millions of Chinese gulping down all that rice, you know that China just has to be the world's champion rice-eating nation.

But not all Chinese depend on rice. In the north, the main food is more likely to be wheat. It isn't that northern Chinese have anything against eating rice. It's just that they can't always get it, or get enough of it.

The point is that the Chinese nation is a huge society that is not "all alike." Within China there are great differences in geographical conditions and climate. Among the Chinese there are wide variations in speech, customs, and habits.

A country that does things backward. That depends on your own idea of the "right way" to perform a certain task, based on your own customs and habits. Some Chinese customs do seem to be the exact opposite of customs in the Western world. But there are also many Chinese customs that would seem perfectly "normal" to anyone anywhere in the world.

What differences there are stem largely from the fact that China developed as a distinctly separate civilization. Its traditions were, for the most part, refined over many centuries with relatively little borrowing from other societies. In fact, the past rulers of China showed little or no interest in any other nations of the world.

Because Chinese civilization is one of the world's oldest, many people think of China as "unchanging." This view has been badly shattered in our own time. From the start, the government of the People's Republic denounced many of China's traditional ways and made an all-out effort to change them. Yet the length and strength of this campaign showed how deeply the old ways were rooted. Moreover, in their drive to change China, the Communists sometimes used methods that seemed to stem from ancient tradition.

No wonder, then, if outsiders have a cloudy picture of China. It is a nation that has gone through more changes than almost any other, and is still far from settled. At the same time, it is a nation that carries the legacy of one of the world's oldest civilizations.

What happens in China can have a lasting impact not only on the millions of Chinese but on everyone in the world. That's why it is important for us to make our picture of China as sharp and clear as we can. To do this, we must look beyond the events of the day. We need to search out the forces and conditions, the values and beliefs, which have made China what it is and the Chinese the way they are.

1
THE LAND AND PEOPLE

Chapter 1

The Land

UNLESS YOU ARE among Chinese who can speak English, you will never hear them call their own country "China" or call themselves "Chinese." They call their country *Chung-kuo,** meaning the "Middle Kingdom" (or in a more up-to-date translation, the "Central Country"). And they call themselves the *Chung-kuo jen,** or "people of the Central Country."

And if you look at a map of the Asian continent, it is easy to see what is central about China. First, China is, in area, the largest country entirely in Asia. Second, China sits right in the heartland of Asia, bordered on three sides by the other countries of the continent, and, at the same time, cut off from them by some of the world's highest mountains. On the fourth side, to the east, lies the vast Pacific.

---

*See the Spelling and Pronunciation Guide for all starred words. This book uses the traditional spelling of Chinese words and names, but the new spellings are given in the guide.

✌§ China's great rivers are givers of life. But they can also take it away.

Some people — with good imaginations — have said that China is shaped like a large cat, its paws and legs tucked up under its body, resting on a bed of nails. To these people, the northeastern area known as Manchuria juts out to form the cat's "head." The area called Inner Mongolia becomes the "neck" and "swayback" of the cat, and the rest of China is the round, plumpish body. The "bed of nails" on which the cat rests is the Himalaya mountain range, which includes Mount Everest, the world's highest peak.

Not only is China the biggest among all countries which are located entirely in Asia, it is also the third largest country in the world. Only the Soviet Union and Canada are larger. The United States is slightly smaller. If you could somehow pick up China and drop it on top of the 48 mainland states of the United States, a little piece of China would overlap into Canada in the northeast and part of southern China would plop into the Gulf of Mexico.

☆　☆　☆　☆　☆　☆　☆　☆　☆

Where people live greatly influences *how* they live. China's broad, often harsh landscape has left deep imprints on Chinese habits and attitudes, on the way the people of China live, and on the way they view the world.

For example, for thousands of years, many of the rivers of China have overflowed their banks and brought fresh, new topsoil to the land every year. Because of this, the bulk of China's farmers have always lived near its rivers. Also, since the great rivers of China can be traveled by boats for long distances,

16

*Six out of every seven Chinese live along the
banks of rivers. Above, a farmer poles his
sampan, a kind of boat, up Kwei River.*

most of the inland cities, the trading centers, are situated along the rivers.

On the other hand, the tall mountains and forbidding deserts of northern and western China make these areas almost impossible to live in. Here, in the region known as the "empty lands," a traveler might run into some wandering herdsmen, a few isolated towns and cities, and then mile after mile of emptiness.

By contrast the eastern part of China is jammed with people. Here, along the banks of China's great river systems, six out of every seven Chinese live. The great rivers — the Yangtze Kiang,* the Yellow (or

17

Hwang Ho* in Chinese), and the West (Hsi Kiang* in Chinese) — run through country that has fertile land and a temperate climate. Unfortunately only about 15 percent of China's total land area is farmable. What is available is farmed intensely.

Visitors to the Chinese countryside often get the impression that just about every square inch of land that doesn't have a house sitting on it is given over to the plow. In many areas, terraces have been laboriously hacked from the mountainsides to create additional rice fields. Even so, growing enough food and getting it distributed to its large population have always been China's biggest problem.

China's great rivers are givers of life. But they can also take it away. For example, in 3,000 years of recorded history, the Hwang Ho has changed course at least 26 times and has overflowed its banks, causing disastrous floods, about once every two years.

In 1938, to halt an advancing Japanese army, the Chinese deliberately permitted the Hwang Ho to break through its dikes and flood. The Japanese were halted, but there were other results too. Thousands of people were drowned, and six million acres of farmland were turned into a sea of mud. The flood was followed by a famine in which 880,000 people died and six million more were left homeless. It is from events like these that the Hwang Ho got its nickname: "China's sorrow."

The Yangtze, on the other hand, is a kindlier river which hardly ever overflows its banks. It winds its way through China for 3,200 miles from the Tibetan plateau to the East China Sea. It is China's lifeline to the sea, because large ships can travel upstream for nearly a thousand miles. To the south of the Yangtze are some of China's richest farmlands; to the north are China's industries. And located on the Yangtze

CHINA'S PROVINCES
AND AUTONOMOUS REGIONS

HEILUNGKIANG

KIRIN

LIAONING

INNER MONGOLIAN AUTONOMOUS REGION

SINKIANG UIGHUR AUTONOMOUS REGION

KANSU

HOPEH

NINGSIA A.R.

SHANSI

SHANTUNG

TSINGHAI

SHENSI

HONAN

KIANGSU

TIBETAN AUTONOMOUS REGION

ANHWEI

HUPEH

CHEKIANG

SZECHWAN

HUNAN

KIANGSI

FUKIEN

KWEICHOW

YUNNAN

KWANGSI A.R.

KWANGTUNG

To govern China, the Communists have split it up into a number of provinces and "autonomous regions." Members of China's minority groups live mostly in the autonomous regions.

are many of China's major inland cities, the centers of Chinese commerce.

In the south, the waters of the Hsi Kiang connect the inland regions to the coastal city of Canton,* one of China's oldest trading ports. The warm, humid climate of south China, nourished by the rains of the

19

summer monsoon, is ideal for such thirsty crops as rice.

But the monsoon winds which bring moisture from the South China Sea are not very reliable. If the monsoon brings too much rain, the rivers sometimes flood and drown the crops. If the monsoon arrives too late or is too weak, the crops will die and there may be famine.

☆　☆　☆　☆　☆　☆　☆　☆　☆

The vastness of China and its rugged terrain tended to keep people in one part of China apart from people in another. Even with an expanding railroad network and airline service in recent years, people in different parts of the country have gone their own ways, developing their own customs and habits. In the past, Chinese living in one province have been known to describe their fellow Chinese in the next province as "men from other lands."

Similarly, China's natural walls and vast area helped seal it off from the rest of the world in times past. While mountains and deserts guarded the country from invasions, they also stood in the way of friendlier contacts with the people to the north, northwest, and southwest. The Pacific Ocean on the east and southeast served as the biggest barrier of all — until fairly recent times when the Chinese learned the knack of making long ocean voyages.

As a result, the Chinese have been an inward-looking people. Through most of their history they have shown little interest in other people in other places. Because of China's isolation, its society developed in a world of its own. Thus, it is not too surprising that the Chinese came to consider their land as the center of everything. They were, they thought, Chung-kuo, the "Central Country."

Double-check

Review

1. Why do the Chinese call their land the "Central Country"?

2. Which are the only two countries in the world larger in area than China?

3. Why do six out of every seven Chinese live in the eastern part of China?

4. What percentage of China's land is farmable?

5. Why is the Hwang Ho River called "China's sorrow"?

Discussion

1. This chapter points out that *where* people live influences *how* they live. List the ways this is true for *your* community. Then compare your list with the information about China in the chapter. Would it make sense to say, "Geography is destiny"? Why, or why not?

2. Rivers play a significant role in the life of China. Are they more important in this respect than rivers in the United States? Explain your answer.

3. In the past, Chinese people from different provinces referred to each other as "men from other lands." Do you think such provincialism still exists in China? In the U.S.? What could or should governments do to overcome such attitudes?

Activities

1. A committee of students might be formed to prepare a large wall map of China for use with this and future chapters. They could use the map on page 6 as a guide, and then add information to it from other maps, including others in this book.

2. Six Chinese words in Chapter 1 are starred (*). This indicates that they are in the Spelling and Pronunciation Guide at the back of the book. The names of the provinces on the map in this chapter are also in the guide. A committee of students might assume primary responsibility for teaching fellow students how to pronounce these words. They could do this, in advance, for all future chapters.

3. The photo essays near the center of this book contain several photos showing the diversity of the land in China. You might look at those photos now and mark on a map the places they show.

Skills

THE FIVE LONGEST RIVERS IN THE WORLD

River	Length (miles)	Flows into
Nile	4,145	Mediterranean Sea
Amazon	4,000	Atlantic Ocean
Yangtze	3,915	East China Sea
Hwang Ho	2,903	Yellow Sea
Congo	2,900	Atlantic Ocean

Source: *The World Book Encyclopedia*

Use the table above and information in Chapter 1 to answer the following questions.

1. What does this table give information about?
  (a) world lakes (b) China's rainfall (c) world rivers

2. Where did the information in this table come from?
  (a) Chapter 1 (b) *The World Book* (c) China's rulers

3. The Yangtze River flows into what body of water?
  (a) Yellow Sea (b) Atlantic Ocean (c) East China Sea

4. The Hwang Ho River is shorter than the Amazon by how many miles?
  (a) 1,100 (b) 900 (c) 2,900

5. Which two rivers flow into the same body of water?
  (a) Yangtze and Hwang Ho (b) Amazon and Yangtze
  (c) Amazon and Congo

Chapter 2

Who Are the Chinese?

THOUGH NO ONE KNOWS exactly how many people there are in China today, most estimates give China more than one-fifth of the world's total human population. Or, put another way, one person among every five living on this planet is Chinese. Each year, China's population increases by somewhere between 13 and 20 million, depending on the estimate. In other words, China each year adds a population the size of New York, Chicago, and Los Angeles, with perhaps Philadelphia, Detroit, Houston, Baltimore, and Dallas thrown in.

Just where the Chinese people originally came from is something about which modern-day scholars don't agree. Ancient Chinese legend, on the other hand, has no doubt.

According to Chinese legend, the universe was the creation of a dwarflike creature called P'an-ku.* According to the legend, P'an-ku, with hammer and chisel, carved out the sun, the moon, the stars, and the earth. This heroic bit of work seems to have proved most healthy to P'an-ku, as the legend tells us that P'an-ku grew six feet taller with each passing day.

After about 18,000 years of steady chipping and a lot of growing, P'an-ku finally finished his work and, understandably, collapsed from exhaustion. In death his head became the mountains, his blood the rivers, his breath the winds, his voice the rolling thunder, his flesh the soil, his bones the rocks and metals in the earth.

And people? According to some versions of the P'an-ku myth, human beings sprang from the fleas which had plagued poor old P'an-ku throughout his life. Ancient Chinese myth-makers, it seems, held a rather low opinion of mankind.

Modern-day Chinese scholars regard the story of P'an-ku as one of the most amusing of the old Chinese legends. Still, modern scholarship has yet to provide a definite explanation for just who the Chinese are and where they came from — at least one on which all scholars can agree.

Some scholars insist that the Chinese must be descended from the very first human inhabitants of East Asia. Others believe that the Chinese moved into their homeland from someplace else during some unrecorded era long ago. The place where they came from is usually thought to be to the west of China, possibly in central Asia. There is even one theory that the early Chinese might have been directly related to the ancient Egyptians or Babylonians, though most scholars now doubt that.

Still others argue that the Chinese we. e probably not descended from any single racial stock. They believe that many Asian groups and tribes began a process of meeting and mixing a long time ago. According

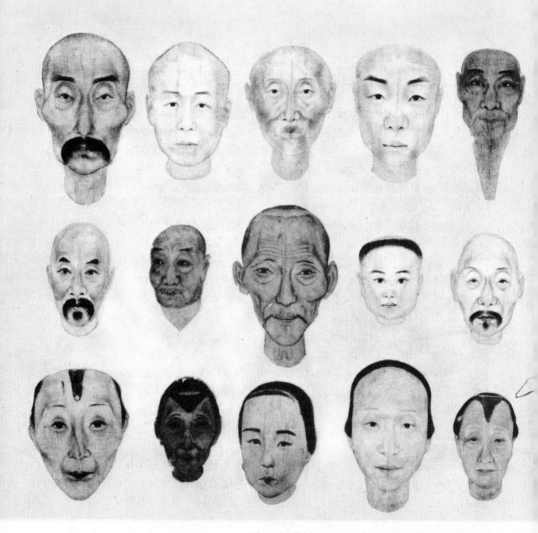

An old Chinese scroll portrays a number of different Chinese facial types. What point, if any, do you think the artist was trying to make?

to this line of thinking, the Chinese as they are known today represent the result of thousands of years of intermingling.

Who's right? So far there isn't enough evidence to prove any of these theories. Perhaps the origin will always remain a mystery.

Whatever the case, about 95 percent of China's present population is made up of people called *Han**Chinese. They are named after the Han dynasty which ruled China for about 400 years and helped mold many of the characteristics of Chinese society today. The remaining five percent of China's population is made up of people who speak various languages and have customs that set them apart from the majority Han Chinese.

These include peoples known as Mongols,* Chuang,* Tibetans,* Manchus,* and Uigurs.* Although these peoples are not Chinese, they are almost all closely related to the Chinese. Most of them live in border areas in the southwest, west, and northwest of China.

As we have seen, the Chinese have long formed the largest group among the Asian, or Mongoloid, peoples, one of the three major branches of the human race. (The other branches are Caucasoid or "white" and Negroid or "black.") The vast majority of the people of China belong to the Mongoloid group. So too do most of the people of East and Southeast Asia.

Most Mongoloids and almost all Chinese have some or all of the following physical features: relatively flat facial features, dark eyes shaped like almonds, light brown or yellow skin, straight black hair. Yet some Han Chinese have few of these characteristics, and some have none. So if physical looks do not set the Chinese apart from other Asians, what does?

In part it is the customs and values of the Chinese. In part it is the language. And in part it is that very hard-to-describe thing known as a "sense of identity." All of these features are the heritage of a great civilization which began taking root more than 35 centuries ago.

"The biggest construction job in Chinese history": The Great Wall stretches on and on across the hills of northern China.

REACHING FOR EMPIRE

LIKE OTHER GREAT ANCIENT CIVILIZATIONS — those of ancient Egypt, Mesopotamia, India, for example — early Chinese society grew up on the fertile plains and valleys of a great river system. In China's case it was the Yellow (Hwang Ho) River and several smaller rivers which fed into the Yellow. Because these rivers flooded their banks every year, the fertility of the soil around them was regularly renewed. And because these regions were relatively treeless, there was no need to hack down great forests to clear the land for planting.

Sometime during the mists of time, the early Chinese people began working the soil with primitive stone tools. They learned how to tame animals — oxen, pigs, dogs, sheep, and horses. They learned how to fashion pots from clay. Why was this important? Because with pots, people could store their food and water for future use. They no

27

longer had to constantly hunt to feed themselves, nor did they have to run down to the river each time they became thirsty.

Since their primitive farming methods brought little return, we can assume that the early Chinese depended to a large degree on sharing and cooperation to survive. Members of immediate families joined with their relatives to form larger families — or clans. Then two or more neighboring clans might pool their resources and labor to form a tribal organization. Two or more neighboring tribes might agree to an alliance for their common defense against other hostile tribes. In this way, the early Chinese societies along the Yellow River grew into increasingly complex social units.

The story of the Chinese in prehistoric times is sketchy at best. In fact, most of what we know today about those long-ago eras comes from discoveries made in relatively recent times. New finds are still being made from time to time to change or modify our picture of prehistoric China.

The first leaders of China of which we have actual evidence are the rulers of the Shang* dynasty. (A dynasty is a succession of rulers from a single family.) Some Chinese historians have argued that Shang government was based on a system of slavery. While there is no solid proof of this, records of that period do tell of cruel customs. To appease the spirit world, for example, the Shang rulers sometimes made human sacrifices. The hapless victims in these ceremonies were usually war captives.

By Shang times, about 1800 B.C., the wheel had been invented and the horse harnessed. Shang chieftains clanked into battle on chariots drawn by two- or four-horse teams, much in the style of the warrior heroes of ancient Greece. The Shang were also skilled craftsmen. Beautifully cast bronze urns, jugs, and bowls dating from the Shang dynasty have recently been dug from the ground. The Shang had also worked out a fairly accurate calendar. No doubt this scientific way of counting the days was a big help to farmers in determining the times to begin plowing and planting.

In a pattern often repeated in China's long history, the royal house of Shang rose, reached a peak of power, and then began a downhill slide to defeat. Tradition tells us that the last Shang king in the 12th century B.C. was a drunk, hated by his oppressed subjects. But since his successors started this tradition, the last Shang king might well have been a victim of slander.

The next of the great Chinese dynasties, the Chou,* [Zhou] saw their rule evaporate into a period of turmoil which the Chinese call the Era of the Warring States. Surprisingly, for all this turmoil this was one of the most productive periods for cultural advancements in Chinese history. In part because there was so much social confusion, some of the best minds of the time began trying to figure out what was wrong with human society. Among the great philosophers of this period were Confucius,* Mencius,* and Lao-tzu,* each of whom contributed his own ideas on the individual and society (see Chapters 3 and 4).

The Warring States stopped warring only when one of them defeated all the others and thereby ran out of organized opposition. The winner of this early Chinese eliminations tournament was the state called Ch'in.* [Quin]

It was during this dynasty, beginning in the third century B.C., that the Western world first began to take note of this far-off country. And today most of the outside world still knows that nation as China, a variation of the name Ch'in. [Quin]

The victorious king of Ch'in [Quin] believed that he had created a new empire that would last forever and gave himself the title of Shih Huang-ti,* the First Emperor. He expected that his successors would number themselves after him (Second Emperor, Third Emperor, etc.).

The armies of Shih Huang-ti fanned out over much of what is today regarded as China. But the troublesome "barbarian" tribes to the north remained the greatest threat to his empire. This threat led to the biggest construction job in Chinese history: the Great Wall of China.

Actually sections of the wall had been built in earlier times. Shih Huang-ti now ordered them connected. To do

SHANG DYNASTY
(About 1800 B.C.-1123 B.C.)

ZHOU DYNASTY
(1123 B.C.-256 B.C.)

the job, whole armies of laborers were forced to work on the project. Many thousands must have died in the effort. But on completion only a few years later, the Wall stretched nearly 1,500 miles in an unbroken line, with sturdy watchtowers placed every few hundred yards.

The Great Wall did not do what it was supposed to do (protect the Chinese to the south from the nomadic tribes to the north). In centuries to come, the northern nomads would often breach the Wall and invade China. Still, the Great Wall remains to this day the biggest hunk of man-made masonry ever put on earth.

Shih Huang-ti died in 210 B.C., after only 11 years on the throne. His "universal and everlasting empire" survived only four more years after his death.

The next dynasty — the Han dynasty — produced one of the most brilliant periods in China's history. With only one brief interruption, the Han emperors ruled China for more than 400 years, from 206 B.C. to 220 A.D. By coincidence this was almost precisely the period when the Roman Empire in Europe attained the height of its glory. Though these two great empires were similar in size and power, each was only dimly aware of the other's existence. Wealthy Romans prized the silks of China brought West by camel caravan along the Silk Road, a long, arduous trek through the desolate lands of central Asia. In return the Romans sent glass, horses, ivory, and woolen and linen cloth to China.

Quin

CHIN DYNASTY
(221 B.C.-206 B.C.)

HAN DYNASTY
(206 B.C.-220 A.D.)

China's ancient dynasties: Where did China's civilization arise? In what directions did the dynasties expand? Why?

But beyond that, contacts between the two regions were few. For most practical purposes, the distances involved were simply too great for the transportation and communications of those times.

The Han Empire covered most of East Asia. In the northeast, Han generals pushed the borders of empire into what is today Korea. In the south, Han domains extended into Vietnam. In the interior, Han authority reached into the center of the Asian continent.

With the expansion of territory came a surge in wealth and population within Han China. The arts and scholarship flourished, aided by the invention of paper which helped to spread the written word. The ideas of Confucius (*see* Chapter 3) were established as national doctrine. To administer the vast empire, a large civil service system was formed, manned by scholars recommended by local officials.

Most important, a pattern of Chinese life jelled during the Han era and became one of the most enduring social systems yet devised by man. In the centuries following the fall of the Han dynasty in 220 A.D., China frequently fell into times of chaos. New ruling dynasties rose and fell. Foreign conquerors came and went. But the basic Chinese traditions remained, lasting into the modern era.

Double-check

Review

1. What portion of the world's population lives in China?

2. What percentage of China's population is Han Chinese?

3. Name three minority groups living in China.

4. What is a dynasty?

5. When and why did Westerners come to call Asia's "Central Country" *China*?

6. What was the Great Wall of China supposed to do?

Discussion

1. This chapter briefly describes the P'an-ku myth about the origin of China and its earliest inhabitants. Can such myths contain "truths" even if the events they describe might not have happened? What does the P'an-ku myth tell us about ancient Chinese attitudes toward the forces of nature and the relationship of humans to those forces? Does the humor "hurt" or "help" the message?

2. What would you say to correct someone who said, "All Chinese look alike"? Do you think that to some Chinese all white and/or black people look alike? What — other than prejudice — might cause such attitudes? What dangers are there in believing such things? How are such attitudes changed?

3. Some Chinese traditions established 2,000 years ago have lasted into modern times. How could these traditions have been passed down through the years? What U.S. traditions do you think will last 2,000 years?

Activities

1. Some students might illustrate the P'an-ku myth with a series of drawings for bulletin board display.

2. The photos throughout this text might be examined for examples of the Chinese facial types illustrated in the old scroll shown in this chapter.

3. Several student committees might be formed to research and report to the rest of the class on some of the following topics: Other Civilizations' Creation Myths; The Latest Findings and Theories About the Origins of China's First Inhabitants; Construction of the Great Wall; Similarities and Differences Between the Han Dynasty and the Roman Empire.

Skills

DISTRIBUTION OF THE WORLD'S POPULATION

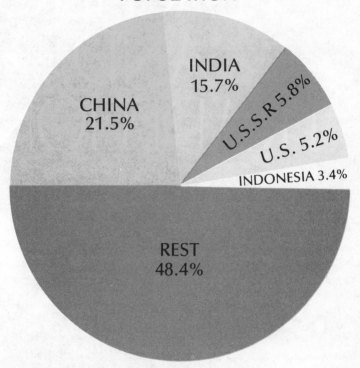

Source: Population Reference Bureau, 1984

Use the circle graph above and information in Chapters 1 and 2 to answer the following questions.

1. This chart shows the percentage of people who live in various
a) worlds   b) hemispheres   c) countries

2. Which country has the largest population?
a) India   b) China   c) U.S.S.R.

3. What share of the world's people lives in China?
a) less than one tenth   b) almost one half   c) more than one fifth

4. More than half of the people in the world live in the top
a) two countries   b) four countries   c) five countries

5. On which continent do most of the people in the world live?
a) Africa   b) South America   c) Asia

2
TEACHERS
AND
TRADITIONS

Chapter 3

What Confucius Really Said

HE NEVER THOUGHT of himself as a hero or a great scholar. "As to being a Sage or even a Good Man," he said, "far be it from me to make any such claim. [But] as for tireless effort to learn and unflagging patience in teaching others, those are merits that I do not hesitate to claim."

He is known to the Chinese as Kung Fu-tzu,* "Kung" being his family name and "Fu-tzu" a sort of honorary title meaning "Grand Master." The non-Chinese world knows him better by the Latin form of his name and title: Confucius.

Despite his own modest words, Confucius left his imprint on China and its people as no one before or after him has done. His ideas became a nation's ideals; his words its national creed.

Confucius was born on the 27th day of the eighth moon in the 22nd year of the rule of Duke

先師孔子行教像

德侔天地道冠古今
刪述六經垂憲萬世

**Grand Master Kung:
The man the Western
world knows as
Confucius as he is
pictured in an old
Chinese woodcut.**

✍ To Confucius the measure of a man's life was not "how long?" but "how good?"

Hsiang* over the State of Lu.* Scholars with a fondness for figuring such things have determined that he was born in the year 551 B.C., during the late Chou period.

Not very much is known about Confucius' early years. By his own account, he was "without rank and in humble circumstances" in his youth. But some Chinese scholars believe that his circumstances weren't quite as humble as he made them sound.

In any event he set his "heart upon learning" at age 15 and had the time to devote to his studies. We can guess that he was largely self-taught.

Confucius lived during an unhappy period of Chinese history. Feudal lords fought one another constantly in a bloody competition for power. To Confucius human society had fallen into moral decay. The effort to restore an ideal social order became his life's work.

In a career of study and teaching that spanned more than 40 years, Confucius edited the best of the ancient Chinese writings. Beyond book learning, Confucius emphasized other skills to produce an early Chinese version of the well-rounded, educated gentleman. The Six Arts of Confucius listed ritual, music, mathematics, history, archery, and a kind of ancient driver-training course for charioteers.

In his time education was mainly for the rich. Children of the ruling aristocrats were taught by private tutors or trained for their life roles by government officials.

Confucius, perhaps remembering his own background, would have none of that. He accepted students on the basis of their desire to learn, not on their social standing or ability to pay. "From the very poorest upward — beginning even with the man who could bring no better present than a bundle of dried meat — none has ever come to me without receiving instruction. Only one who bursts with eagerness do I instruct; only one who bubbles with excitement do I enlighten."

He was one of the most effective and influential teachers the world has ever seen. Yet, through all of his adult life, Confucius aspired to high office so that he might put some of his ideas into practice. But he was unsuccessful.

For many years Confucius traveled through the various states of China in search of an "ideal ruler" — preferably one who was willing to give a certain experienced teacher an opportunity to become an active statesman. But the jealous lords were not about to turn over the administration of their states to a man whom many thought to be a bit strange at best, and perhaps dangerous.

Confucius died in 479 B.C. His life and ideas would have a tremendous impact on the history of a people. But some 300 more years would have to go by before that became evident.

☆ ☆ ☆ ☆ ☆ ☆ ☆ ☆ ☆

Most of what we now know about Confucius is contained in books called the *Analects** (or Conversations) of Confucius. The *Analects* consist of the collected sayings and proverbs of Confucius assembled by his students after the Master's death. The majority of the paragraphs in the *Analects* begin with the phrase, "The Master said...."

At the heart of the teachings of Confucius is a love for all humanity. His ideal man was one who was courteous, loyal, diligent, and kind. He expected his gentleman to be true to his principles, though he conceded that no human being can be totally faultless.

In Confucius' time, only a person who inherited a high station in society could be considered a "gentleman." But Confucius argued that gentlemen were made, not born. Since a gentleman's noble conduct is acquired through education and self-cultivation, anyone can become a gentleman, regardless of the makeup of his family tree, Confucius said.

Confucius endorsed the ancient Chinese concept of honor and respect for ancestors, parents, and elders. He believed that those who honored their own parents would honor other people's parents and elders and that all the people, ultimately, would honor the head of the national family — the emperor.

Confucius believed that those in authority — from the father in a family to the ruler of the state — bore the main responsibility for setting good examples. If a ruler depended only on official regulations and the threat of punishment to govern his people, Confucius advised, "the people will try to keep out of jail but will have no sense of honor or shame." But if a ruler guided his people by virtue, "the people will have a sense of honor and respect."

Confucius counseled his students to seek moderation in almost everything and to avoid extremes. But he expected them to remain true to their own moral principles, even at the risk of their lives. To Confucius the measure of a man's life was not "how long?" but "how good?"

☆ ☆ ☆ ☆ ☆ ☆ ☆ ☆ ☆

Confucius never thought of himself as a founder of a religion. He simply didn't spend much time pondering such questions as the creation of the universe or the prospects for life after death. Indeed, when a student once asked him to discuss death, Confucius answered: "You cannot understand life. How then can you understand death?"

Yet, after his own passing, the Confucian way of thinking gradually developed into a kind of religious cult. Chinese historical traditions said that the disciples of Confucius "scattered and traveled about among the feudal lords. The greater among them became teachers or [officials]. The lesser were friends and teachers of officials." It seemed that many of the local rulers liked to have "guest scholars" and "resident philosophers" in their courts.

Confucianism's most famous champion was another scholar, now known to us as Mencius (again, this name is the Latinized form of the Chinese Meng-tzu* or "Master Meng"). Partly through the efforts of disciples such as Mencius and others, the teachings of Confucius eventually became the ideals of the Chinese people. Confucian classics became the basic textbooks for the training of rulers and officials. Confucian temples were built in most parts of the country so people could pay homage and make sacrifices to his memory.

The cult of Confucianism lasted through the ages — and waned only with the collapse of the Chinese empire in our own 20th century (see Chapter 14). Yet without the threads of Confucian thought woven all through it, the fabric of Chinese history would have emerged in quite a different pattern.

Chapter 4

Taoism and Buddhism

CONFUCIUS WAS the most influential teacher of the late Chou period. But he wasn't the only one. So many different philosophies flourished during this "golden age of Chinese thought" that the Chinese recall that period as the time of the "hundred schools."

Another of the philosophies of this period that has had a long-lasting impact on Chinese thinking was Taoism.* Its basic ideas were supposedly set down by an ancient sage known as Lao-tzu, the name being the Chinese way of saying "Old Master."

In Chinese the word *Tao** means "the way." To Taoists, the Tao is the ultimate law of the universe, the source of all things, and the natural way things happen.

For example, if something should happen to you and you can't really explain why it happened, you might shrug the whole thing off with the phrase, "Well, that's the way it goes." In so doing, you are expressing the essence of Taoism (whether you know it or not).

41

Because Taoists believe that there is a natural course of events that controls everything, they believe in doing as little as possible to change the way things are. By accepting the way things are, people remain in harmony with the natural laws. By seeking to change things, people get out of step with nature and get themselves into a lot of trouble.

Taoists sometimes explain their ideas by using the illustration of water. Water, they point out, has no natural shape of its own but always takes the shape of that which surrounds it (be it a bottle or a riverbank or whatever). Water is a soft substance. Yet over time, it will wear away the hardest rock. And left to itself, water will always seek to find its own natural level.

Thus, true Taoists see no point in trying to improve on nature, in striving for honors, or in acquiring possessions. "He who has the most possessions is he who will lose most heavily. But he who is content is invulnerable," observed Lao-tzu. So if human ambition is self-defeating in the end, why bother with it? Instead, said Lao-tzu, "to possess everything, desire to possess nothing. To be everything, desire to be nothing."

Like Confucianism, Taoism began as a relatively simple philosophy — one man's approach to life. And like Confucianism, Taoism underwent sharp changes in the centuries after it began. It borrowed heavily from old Chinese folk religions, legends, and superstitions. It became a formal religion with a priesthood, temples, monasteries, and elaborate rituals. Many Taoist teachers claimed magical powers for healing the sick, for prolonging life, for predicting the future.

These qualities of later Taoism made it a religion with lots of appeal to the common people of China. With the coming of the scientific age in modern times,

Six hundred years ago, a Chinese artist painted this peaceful scene entitled "Sage Viewing the Moon." In what ways does the painting reflect the beliefs and values of the religion of Taoism?

however, Taoism as a faith skidded into sharp decline. But its ideals of individual self-expression and of harmony between humans and nature greatly influenced countless Chinese artists, poets, and writers down through the ages. Side by side with Confucianism, Taoism helped to mold Chinese society.

☆　☆　☆　☆　☆　☆　☆　☆　☆

The sixth century B.C., the era of Confucius and Lao-tzu, turned out to be a busy time for deep thinkers — not only in China but in other great civilizations of the ancient world. In the West, for example, the

Greek philosopher Pythagoras* was trying to figure out a way to express, through numbers, the makeup of the universe.

In India, a prince-turned-philosopher founded one of the world's great religions, Buddhism. Its founder, Siddhartha Gautama,* was the son of a ruler of one of the smaller states in northern India (in what is today Nepal).

As a young man, Gautama lived a very sheltered life. He experienced only pleasure. His life-style supposedly included the ownership of three palaces — one for the hot season, one for the cold season, and one for the rainy season. He had a beautiful wife, a son, and apparently no problems.

One day, though, Gautama disobeyed his father by leaving one of his palaces to see the real world. He discovered that most other people didn't live the way he did. Indeed, he found misery and suffering everywhere. For the first time he saw the poor, the sick, the starving. The experience left him thoroughly shaken.

At the age of 29 the prince gave up his title, renounced his luxuries — and even his family — to go into the world as a wandering holy man. For the next six years, he traveled, he fasted, he thought, he studied with Hindu scholars — but he failed to find his answer to the meaning of life. Then one day, while sitting and thinking under a tree, he suddenly found the answer. Henceforth he was known as the Buddha* — "the Enlightened One."

In his very first sermon, Buddha summarized his philosophy: Suffering is universal, the cause of suffering is selfish desire, and an escape from suffering can come only by eliminating desires. But by replacing selfishness with kindliness, patience, and pity, the

Head shaved, swathed in robes, young Buddhist monk says morning prayers in Peking temple.

person is rewarded by *Nirvana** or tranquil peace.

Buddhism spread quickly through most of India and became the dominant religion there for several centuries. Thereafter, it declined gradually so that today it is all but extinct in the land of its origin. But Buddhism in various forms spread to many lands in East and Southeast Asia where it firmly established itself.

Scholars believe that Buddhism was introduced in China sometime during the first century A.D. but did not establish itself there right away. Confucianists and Taoists scorned it as some kind of "foreign barbarian idea." Eventually, however, Buddhism proved to be one of the few foreign imports to leave a lasting impact on China. From about the third century on, Buddhism became widespread among the Chinese.

For many centuries these three schools of thought — Confucianism, Taoism, and Buddhism — competed for converts in the general population. Ultimately, however, all three of them settled down to exist side by side with one another. Each began to borrow ideas from the others — and to absorb many of the popular ancient Chinese beliefs and traditions. Over hundreds of years, the three philosophies became so intermixed that they could hardly be separated in the lives of the Chinese.

Thus people did not describe themselves as Confucianist, or Taoist, or Buddhist. Instead many Chinese followed all three schools of thought (or any combination of the three) at the same time. For the Chinese have never had the concept of a single "true religion" to the exclusion of all other faiths. "Good words should be listened to with respect from whatever source they come," goes an old Chinese saying, expressing the tolerance of the Chinese for all religions and different ideas.

Double-check

Review

1. List the Six Arts of Confucius.

2. What are the *Analects*?

3. What does the Chinese word *Tao* mean in English?

4. Which two ideals of Taoism greatly influenced Chinese artists, poets, and writers?

5. What does the word *Buddha* mean in English?

6. What does *Nirvana* mean in English? How does a person achieve it?

Discussion

1. Do you agree with Confucius that those in authority bear the main responsibility for setting good examples? How could this idea be translated into action? Is such a philosophy outdated in modern times? Why, or why not? Do other ideas of Confucius seem appropriate for life today? Which?

2. What are some of the significant similarities and differences between Confucianism, Taoism, and Buddhism?

3. After centuries of "competition," these three schools of thought began to borrow ideas from each other, and many Chinese people practiced all three. Does such a development seem possible with Western religions? If not, why not? If so, what form might such developments take? Explain your answers.

Activities

1. One student might play the role of Confucius applying for a high government position in ancient China. Three other students could play the roles of province officials questioning him about his ideas and qualifications. Afterward, the whole class might decide which — if any — position Confucius should be given.

2. Some students might research and report to the rest of the class biographical information about Confucius, Lao-Tzu, and Buddha.

3. A scholar from a local Chinese community or nearby university might be invited to speak to the class about differences and similarities between Eastern and Western approaches to religion and philosophy.

Skills

USING AN INDEX

Use the index page above and information in Chapters 3 and 4 to answer the following questions.

1. In what order are topics listed in an index?
(a) order of importance   (b) page numbers   (c) alphabetical order

2. On which page would you find an illustration of Chinese calligraphy?
(a) page 64   (b) page 65   (c) page 131

3. On how many pages in this text is Buddhism mentioned?
(a) four pages   (b) five pages   (c) 202 pages

4. On which page would you find the first mention of the Conversations of Grand Master Kung?
(a) page 104   (b) page 105   (c) page 38

5. Which subtopic shown on this index page describes the subject matter of Chapters 3 and 4?
(a) people   (b) religion   (c) daily life

Chapter 5

The Art of Writing

MORE THAN ANYTHING ELSE, the written Chinese language has been the key unifying force in Chinese history. Though the way of writing Chinese has changed greatly since the original forms were invented, the basic principles of China's writing system have remained constant almost from the beginning.

Thus, unlike many other kinds of ancient writing systems, the ancient language of the Chinese never became a "dead language." Through continuous development, Chinese writing has survived through the ages and is still in daily use today.

And unlike most other written languages, written Chinese does not use an alphabet. Instead Chinese writing consists of an enormous collection of symbols — or "characters" — each of which stands for some idea or thing.

The Chinese writing system grew out of an ancient kind of picture-writing. At first the picture words looked very much like the object they were supposed to be picturing. The word for "moon," for instance, took the shape of a crescent moon 月 . Eventually over many centuries, the word "moon" evolved into its present form 月 . Similarly other words have changed in form.

Drawing pictures as words works only up to a point. The Chinese soon discovered that one can't draw simple pictures to indicate more complicated ideas. How, for example, can you draw simple pictures to suggest such ideas as "a month's time," or "peace," or "shining bright"?

Several ways were devised to overcome this sticky problem. One way is to extend the meaning of a word to a related idea. Since the moon goes through all its phases in a month's time, the Chinese word for "moon" can also mean "month," depending on how it's used in a sentence. This idea shouldn't be too mystifying for English-speakers, since our own word "month" comes from the word "moon."

Another common way is to combine two or more picture words to create an idea word. For example, the sun and the moon are the brightest objects in the sky. So combine the two words and you get the Chinese word meaning "bright."

Even in the early days of the Shang dynasty, some 3,000 individual Chinese written characters were in use. By Han times, the word list had between 9,000 and 10,000 characters. A standard Chinese dictionary of our time lists about 50,000 characters, though many of them are rarely used.

How many written characters do you have to know in order to be literate in the written Chinese language? If you were a high school student in China, you would probably be able to recognize some 3,000 to 4,000 individual characters. With this number, you

---

would be able to read a daily newspaper and understand pretty well what it says. A well-educated adult might know twice as many characters, and a highly trained Chinese scholar would be able to read several thousand more.

To build up a reading vocabulary, students of written Chinese must learn the words and commit them to memory through practice, practice, and more practice. If a student should forget how a certain word is written, there is no easy way to "figure it out." He will just have to learn that word all over again. Which brings us to some of the peculiarities of the Chinese language — as it is spoken.

The written Chinese language is uniform for all parts of China. But since the written Chinese characters do not in themselves suggest how these words are to be pronounced, people in different parts of the country do not speak Chinese exactly the same way.

These regional speech variations are called *dialects*. In general the spoken Chinese language may be grouped into seven major dialects. But within these there are hundreds of subdialects or regional variations.

About half of all the people who speak Chinese speak some form of the Mandarin* dialect. When Mandarin speakers from different parts of China meet, their situation is much like that which arises when an American who speaks with the clipped accent of New England meets another American who speaks with a deep Southern drawl. Each may think the other "talks sort of funny," but they have no difficulty talking with one another — most of the time.

Other spoken languages of China are something else again. In the southeastern coastal region, there are six major groups of languages. These groups differ from Mandarin and among themselves to about the degree that English differs from German, and German from Dutch, Dutch from Swedish, and so forth. A Chinese who speaks only one of the languages usually cannot understand another Chinese who speaks a different language.

But whatever the language, there are a number of basic patterns that make up all forms of spoken Chinese. To begin with, almost all of the root words in spoken Chinese are of one syllable, or one sound.

People who have bothered to count all the sounds in Mandarin Chinese report that there are 420 separate ones. Yet, as we already noted, the written Chinese language has about 40,000 to 50,000 separate words. Obviously, with many words and so few sounds, many Chinese words sound very much alike.

Because of this, tones are extremely important. The meaning of a spoken Chinese word depends not only on what word you use but also on how you say it. The sound "shih" in Mandarin, for instance, can mean "history," "city," "lion," "teacher," "the number 10," "to recognize," and a few other things. It depends on how you say "shih" and how the word is used.

In Mandarin Chinese there are four basic tones (some of the other dialects have up to eight tones). To see how the four tones work, think how you might say the word "yes."

The first tone is flat. Suppose someone asked you if your name is John. If it is, you say simply, "Yes."

The second tone rises, as if you are asking a question. If your mother calls you, you reply, "Yes?"

The third tone is like the second, only longer. It

Learning to read in an "outdoor school."
How does this school compare with yours? Do
you think it would be difficult to learn in
such a setting? Or is learning unconnected
with the physical setting of a classroom?

starts high, drops down, then rises again. If someone should say something you don't really believe, you might question him with a doubtful, "Ye-es?" — as if to say, "Oh, yeah?"

The fourth tone resembles the sound of a sharp command. When your teacher gives you a homework assignment and you ask, "Do I have to do it?" and the teacher insists, "Yes!" — you have just been given a fine example of the fourth tone.

There is one important difference between the use of tones in English and in Chinese, however. In English, no matter how you say "yes," it still means "yes" in some way. In Chinese, a change in tone usually changes the meaning of the word entirely. For example:

The sound *chi** said in the first tone means "chicken."

When said in the second tone, it is the verb "to worry."

When said in the third tone, it means "self."

When said in the fourth tone, it becomes the verb "to remember."

The Chinese are extremely proud of their language system. To the Chinese the written Chinese characters are especially pleasing to the eye. And though the differences in spoken Chinese tend to divide the Chinese people into regional and local groupings, the written language provides the Chinese with their strongest bond to their long cultural past.

But even Chinese scholars concede that there are certain difficulties with the language. Learning to read and write it is an extremely time-consuming process. Most Chinese, busy in meeting the needs of daily survival, simply have not had enough time left over to master the language.

Efforts to spread literacy in China in more recent times have brought attempts to simplify the written Chinese script. On mainland China unnecessary written strokes have been lopped off more than 1,000 written words. At the same time, the Chinese government is pushing the use of the Western alphabet alongside the traditional characters (see pages 222-223).

Today Chinese is recognized on the international scene as one of the five official working languages of the United Nations (the other four: English, French, Russian, and Spanish). And to this day more people communicate in the Chinese language than in any other language in the world. The reason is simply that the Chinese form the largest single group in the world and they, of course, use their language all the time.

Double-check

Review

1. What has been the key unifying force throughout China's history?

2. What does written Chinese use in place of an alphabet?

3. Name one way a simple picture word can be used to express a more complex idea.

4. Which Chinese dialect is most commonly used?

5. Describe one important difference in the use of tones in spoken Chinese and in spoken English.

Discussion

1. This chapter calls the written Chinese language "the key unifying force in Chinese history." Based on what you have learned in previous chapters, why has the written language been so important? Is this true of languages in other countries? Explain your answers.

2. What about the effects of the *spoken* language on China's history? What effects do you think it might have had on China's relationships with the rest of the world? On China's approach to education? On China's social and political structures?

3. What do you think causes the development of regional dialects?

Activities

1. The class might be divided into four or five small groups. Each group could think of a short sentence in English and then put the sentence into picture words. When each group is ready, one of its members could draw the picture-word sentence on the board, and the rest of the class could try to translate it back into English.

2. Someone who speaks both Chinese and English might be invited to speak to the class and illustrate the use of tones in spoken Chinese.

3. Some students might research and report to the rest of the class on the regions in China in which each of the seven major Chinese dialects are spoken. This could be shown on a large wall map of China.

Skills

PERCENTAGES OF CHINA'S POPULATION
THAT SPEAK THE MAIN DIALECTS

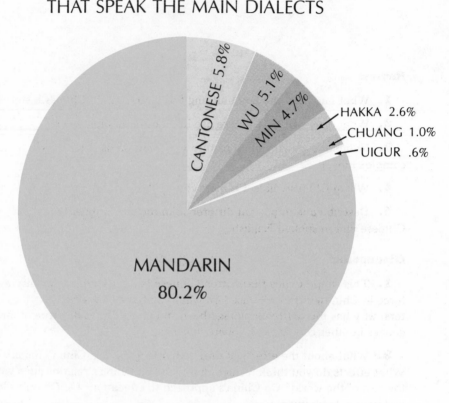

Source: *The World Almanac:* Sidney S. Culbert, Associate Professor of Psychology,
University of Washington

Use the circle graph above and information in Chapter 5 to answer the following questions.

1. How many major dialects are spoken in China?

2. Which dialect do most Chinese people speak?

3. What percentage of Chinese citizens speak the second most common dialect?

4. How do these dialects differ when written?

5. What characteristic of Chinese dialects is similar to dialects in the United States?

Chapter 6

Invented in China

WITH THE FALL OF THE HAN dynasty in 220 A.D., China's first great empire ended. For the next three-and-a-half centuries the country was divided into many rival kingdoms and ruling houses. Then, toward the end of the sixth century A.D., China entered its second great era of empire. Except for a break of about 50 years, two great ruling dynasties, known as the T'ang* and the Sung,* spanned the next 600 years of Chinese history.

The T'ang and Sung periods saw remarkable advances in Chinese science. Three key inventions came into use during that era: movable-type printing, the magnetic compass, and gunpowder.

Actually these ideas didn't just dawn on the Chinese like a bolt out of the blue. They were the results of a long chain of developments with links stretching back thousands of years.

The story of printing, for example, should really begin with the first appearance of paper, which was

*Centuries before it was in use in the West, the
paddle-wheel boat was used in China. This one,
from an old woodcut, was powered mainly by wind.*

invented by the Chinese in the Han period. The Han
Chinese came up with a kind of early printing called
stone rubbings, in which images carved on stone were
transferred onto paper. This was done by pressing a

soft, thin sheet of paper against a stone tablet and then rubbing the paper with lampblack or ink. Wherever the uncarved, or raised, portions of the stone carving pressed against the paper, those portions of the paper turned black. The depressed portions carved into the stone tablet remained white. Thus a black-and-white impression of the stone carving appeared on the paper.

Somewhere down the line, it occurred to the Chinese that you could do the same thing by stamping paper with carved wooden blocks. This kind of block printing, in which an entire page of a book was printed at once, became standard practice by T'ang times. The next step was to have an individual printing block (or "movable" type) for each Chinese character so that a printer could print a variety of words by assembling the proper printing blocks. The movable type was first carved in clay. Later metal type came into use. The first such type came into use in China about 1000 A.D., more than 400 years before the German printer Johann Gutenberg began using the European version of movable type.

The background of the compass is also long. But it was not until the Sung era that the magnetic needle — suspended on a silk thread or floated in a dish of water — was put into wide use for navigation on the high seas. Chinese overseas trade with Japan and Southeast Asia increased greatly during the Sung dynasty. And the compass greatly increased the chances that Chinese sailors, sailing out of sight of land, would find their way to where they were going. It is now believed that Arab seafarers learned of the compass from the Chinese. The Arabs, in turn, passed on this knowledge to Europe.

Exploding powder was probably discovered sometime in the T'ang era and may have been used first in magical ceremonies. But Sung-dynasty generals apparently found the crash and swoosh of exploding fireworks most useful in scaring the horses of the enemy.

The list of inventions and innovations known to the Chinese well before they were known to other people elsewhere is lengthy. These include the crossbow, saddle stirrups, the wheelbarrow, the water-powered spinning wheel, paper money, and paddle-wheel boats. In outstanding engineering feats, apart from the Great Wall, the early seventh century saw the completion of the first Grand Canal, an 850-mile-long man-made waterway linking the Yellow River in the north to the Yangtze in the south.

Not every Chinese scientific, technical, or engineering effort in those early days, of course, turned out to be a whopping success. The Chinese had no better luck than anyone else in seeking a drug for everlasting life or a way to convert cheap metals into gold.

Yet during the T'ang and Sung dynasties, the overall level of science in China was easily as advanced as that of any other civilization of that day, and a lot more advanced than most. The achievements of China during its golden age gave the Chinese a strong sense of pride in the richness of their heritage.

Unfortunately for China's history, the golden age ceased with the end of the Sung dynasty in 1279 A.D. Never again would that burst of creative energy in the Chinese sciences be wholly repeated. The Chinese spirit of inventiveness flagged and withered.

But the Chinese continued to feel that their culture was superior to the cultures of all other peoples — long after the facts supported this attitude. And as it turned out, this gap between belief and reality would one day spell national tragedy. That day came when traditional China was jostled and pushed into the modern age.

*Fourteen centuries ago, Chinese engineers and
laborers combined to build the Grand Canal,
linking the Yellow River and the Yangtze. They
did the job so well that the canal is in use even
today. This painting shows men towing the barge
of a Sung dynasty emperor along the canal.*

A.H.

Double-check

Review

1. When and where was paper invented?

2. About how long before Gutenberg began using movable type in Europe was this printing technique used in China?

3. How did Europeans learn about the use of the compass for navigation purposes?

4. For what purpose was exploding powder probably first used after its invention in China? How was it later used by Sung-dynasty generals?

5. How long is the Grand Canal? What two rivers does it link? How many centuries ago was it completed?

Discussion

1. Of all the Chinese inventions mentioned in this chapter, which one would you say has had the greatest impact on the world? Why? How would you rank the others in order of importance? Give reasons for your choices.

2. What cultural factors might make one society more inventive than another? What might cause one period of a society's history to be highly inventive while other periods, before and after, are not so inventive?

3. Should a culture that is highly inventive be thought of as "superior" to others? Why, or why not? What other things might indicate "superiority" of a culture?

Activities

1. Some students might do the research to conduct a panel discussion for the rest of the class comparing and contrasting the level of technology in China and Europe between 600 A.D. and 1200 A.D.

2. Using thin paper and charcoal or crayons, some students might try some "stone rubbings" of various types, using any hard surface with raised letters or designs on it — manhole covers, for example. Some students might carve block letters on wood or soap and make rubbings of these.

3. Using an actual compass, three students might role-play the parts of a Chinese sailor explaining this new invention to an Arab sailor, who could then explain it to a European sailor.

Skills

CHINESE INVENTIONS

SUNG DYNASTY

HAN DYNASTY

TANG DYNASTY

(a) Exploding powder scares horses

(b) Work begun to build Grand Canal

(c) Compass used for navigation

(d) Books printed from wooden blocks

(e) Paper invented

(f) Exploding powder used for magic

(g) Stone images rubbed onto paper

Use the two lists above and information in Chapter 6 to do the following things on a separate sheet of paper.

1. Across the top of the paper, list the three dynasties in the order in which they occurred. (They are *not* in the correct order above.)

2. Under the name of each dynasty, list the letters of the events that occurred during that dynasty. (The events are *not* in the correct order above.)

Chapter 7

The Arts:
Visions in the "Mind's Eye"

SINCE WRITTEN CHINESE WORDS began as a form of picture-writing, the Chinese consider the written word to be as pretty as a picture. In the very early days, the Chinese gave special magical qualities to the words themselves. But if the magic has faded in the passing centuries, the Chinese still deeply appreciate the beauty in their own writing system.

From this springs the art of calligraphy.* What's that? It is the skill of true penmanship (not to be confused with ordinary handwriting). Good calligraphy need not be especially neat or even readable. But it must have balance, proper proportions, and flow. And it must express the individual style and personality of the artist.

In China the traditional writing instrument has been the writing brush, shaped much like a small paint brush. With the writing brush, the calligrapher can form each word precisely as he wants to. By vary-

獨酌無相親
月既不解飲
行樂須及春
醒時同交歡
相期邈雲漢

DRINKING ALONE IN THE MOONLIGHT

A pot of wine among flowers.
I alone, drinking, without a companion.
I lift the cup and invite the bright moon.
My shadow opposite certainly makes us three.
But the moon cannot drink.
And my shadow follows the motions of my body in vain.
For the briefest time are the moon and my shadow my companions.
Oh, be joyful! One must make the most of Spring.
I sing — the moon walks forward rhythmically;
I dance, and my shadow shatters and becomes confused.
In my waking moments, we are happily blended.
When I am drunk, we are divided from one another and scattered.
For a long time I shall be obliged to wander without intention;
But we will keep our appointment by the far-off Cloudy River.

by Li T'ai-Po

The poem above, a stanza of which is shown at
top, is probably the most famous Chinese poem
ever written. The poet, Li T'ai-Po, lived
12 centuries ago, but his words still are
moving. What is the main idea of the poem?

ing the pressure on the brush he can vary the thickness of each stroke all the way from a fat blob to a sharp point.

Or, as Wang Hsi-chih,* one of China's greatest calligraphers who lived during the fourth century A.D., once described his art: "Every horizontal line is like a mass of clouds in battle form, every hook like a bent bow of great strength, every dot like a falling rock from a high peak, every turning of the stroke like a brass hook, every drawn-out line like a dry vine of great age, and every swift and free stroke like a runner on his start."

An expert writing style has always been a mark of the educated Chinese gentleman. Great samples of the calligrapher's art are admired and cherished as fine paintings (and often hung on the walls of private homes and public buildings as decorations). Young Chinese spend hours and hours practicing their penmanship. Those aspiring to become outstanding calligraphers must spend many years in patient practice.

Since brushwork was already so much a part of the schooling in traditional China, many gentlemen also branched off to painting. Often, indeed, painting and calligraphy were combined in a single work. The words, however, weren't a caption, as they didn't necessarily explain what the picture was all about.

Classical Chinese paintings were most often done on long scrolls of paper on silk panels. The artist did not march out into the countryside with his brushes to paint a scene from direct observation. Instead he painted with his "mind's eye" — a scene that took shape in his own mind.

The Chinese artist did not feel that he must paint his subjects exactly as they might appear in nature. Yet even though the artist took certain liberties, a

*Faces painted, and decked out in colorful and
ornate costumes, two singers of the Peking Opera
act out a historical pageant of Chinese history.*

viewer rarely has any trouble identifying what's in
the picture. People look like people, plants look like
plants.

The Chinese believed that some types of artistic
creation were less important than other types. This

was not necessarily because they required less talent and skill. Rather, it was because some art forms didn't fit as well into old Chinese ideas of what gentlemen-scholars were supposed to do.

Sculpturing, for example, was not considered a major art form. The Chinese thought of statues more as decoration than as pure art. They were frequently used in the service of religion. Marble carvings and bronze castings immortalized gods and goddesses, the Buddha and other saints, and various kinds of real or legendary animals.

Many other arts sprang from folk traditions. These included pottery making, textiles, lanterns, paper cutting, and toy making. Even such things as jade and ivory carving, porcelain ware (still popularly called "chinaware" or just "china" in many parts of the world), or embroidery were considered to be the works of craftsmen rather than of artists in old China. Ironically some of these same samples are thought today to have such artistic and historic value that they are now proudly displayed in museums around the world.

The theater was a highly popular art form and an effective way to reach the masses of the Chinese people who could not read. But no theatrical form attained great stature until the rise of Chinese opera in relatively recent times. Opera in China combines many of the stage arts: acting, singing, orchestral music, dancing, and — unlike Western opera — acrobatics. The actors and actresses wear colorful costumes and portray their roles as much through gestures and postures as through their singing lines. From set patterns in facial makeup, any Chinese opera buff can tell at a glance who are the "good guys" and who are the "bad guys."

And, finally, one other Chinese "art" might be

*Fine cooking has long been an honorable tradi-
tion in China. Here a peasant man prepares a
platter full of meat dumplings for the evening
meal as his wife looks on.*

mentioned: the appreciation of food and fine cooking. This would surely be ranked among the lesser arts since it would be beneath the dignity of a gentleman-scholar to enter a kitchen and bend over a hot stove. Nevertheless, fine cooking was long an honorable and enjoyable tradition of China. Many people, including Confucius, reflected at length on what was fit to eat and drink and what wasn't. Chinese cooking artists developed a wide variety of styles and many out-standing regional specialties. Today many international cooking experts rank Chinese cooking among the finest in the world.

Old Chinese view of a fierce enemy: Mounted on wiry ponies, Mongol archers devastated and conquered much of central Asia.

THE MONGOL EMPIRE

EARLY IN THEIR RECORDED HISTORY, the Chinese came to think of the world as divided mainly into two parts: a civilized part (China) and a barbarian part (the rest of the world).

The Chinese claim to superiority was based on culture. They believed that they were the best of all peoples because they were the owners of a better culture. By this measure, all foreigners were "barbarians," because they were untouched by the civilizing influence of China's culture.

The Chinese were not altogether selfish in their claims of superiority. A foreigner of any race or place of origin could shed the status of "barbarian" and become "civilized" in Chinese eyes. But to do so, the foreigner had to become educated in Confucian classics and accept Chinese manners and traditions.

The "barbarians" most troublesome to the Chinese were the many nomad tribes who inhabited the grassy steppe regions of North and Central Asia. These nomads depended on their herds of grazing animals for their food and livelihood. The harshness of their surroundings and their constant struggle for survival helped to produce a rough and sturdy breed of people.

In the 13th century one of the most successful — and destructive — war machines that the world has ever seen stormed out of the steppe lands of Mongolia and conquered the Chinese. The founder of Mongol power was the chieftain Temujin,* better known to history as Genghis Khan.*

The terrific striking power of his armies came from sharpshooting archers mounted on wiry little Mongolian ponies. Time and again swift-moving columns of Mongol cavalry outrode, outflanked, and outfought their slower-moving enemies. Eventually Genghis Khan united the various tribes and clans of Mongols.

Under Genghis Khan and his successors, Mongol-led forces swept over China, Korea, and across North and Central Asia. In the west, the Mongols (known there as "Tartars") conquered most of Russia and penetrated into Europe as far as what is today Hungary.

In China the Mongol conquest was completed by Kublai Khan,* a grandson of Genghis. The furious assault of the Mongols might have wiped out China and its civilization forever. Whole cities and populations were put to the fire and sword. Sometimes the cruel reputation of the Mongols was enough to make their terrified opponents give up without a struggle.

Yet in his way, Kublai Khan was an enlightened emperor. He did much to promote trade and to restore a measure of prosperity and peace to his empire. A lover of splendor, he built a magnificent capital near the present site of Peking.

Since the Mongol conquest had united a vast area from China almost to the shores of the Mediterranean Sea, the entire region was opened to travelers. Despite the hazards of such a long journey, many people from distant lands found their way to China.

The most famous of them was a young man from Ven-

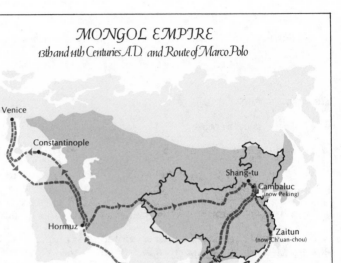

MONGOL EMPIRE
13th and 14th Centuries A.D. and Route of Marco Polo

Venice

Constantinople

Shang-tu

Cambaluc
(now Peking)

Hormuz

Zaitun
(now Ch'uan-chou)

Pagan

▪▪▪▪▪ Marco Polo Route
―――― China's Borders Today

At its height, Mongol empire spread from which great ocean into which present-day countries on north, south, and west?

ice named Marco Polo. With his father and uncle, he arrived in China (or Cathay, as he called it) in 1275 and lived there for the next 17 years, many of them as an official of the empire.

After the Polos returned to Europe, Marco Polo dictated an account of his far-flung adventures. At first few believed his tales. But in time his report helped to open European eyes to the riches of the East and to spur new efforts to establish links to the distant Orient.

Meanwhile Mongol power began to disintegrate in China after Kublai Khan's death in 1294. A series of weak Mongol emperors could not check the flames of revolt that engulfed south China and gradually spread northward. In 1368 Chinese rebels expelled the last of the hated Mongol overlords. The Mongols had ruled China for a little more than a century — which is a relatively short time in the history of this ancient country.

Double-check

Review

1. What is calligraphy?

2. What has been the traditional writing instrument in China?

3. Why did the Chinese believe that some types of artistic creation were less important than other types?

4. Who was Temujin? What clans and tribes did he unite?

5. What Mongolian leader completed the conquest of China? How long did the Mongols then rule China?

6. Who was Europe's most famous explorer of 13th-century China?

Discussion

1. This chapter points out that in traditional China some types of artistic creation were less important than other types. Do you agree with this point of view? Why, or why not? What — if any — are the differences between "art" and "decoration"? What are the differences between "arts" and "crafts"?

2. Is cooking thought of as an art today? Should it be? Would more men cook if it were treated as an art? Explain your answers.

3. Could it be said that in the long run China benefited from the Mongol invasion? If so, how? If not, why not?

Activities

1. Some students might try to write "calligraphic" versions of the English alphabet and post them on the bulletin board. Some might write poems in this style.

2. Some, or all, members of the class might take field trips to nearby museums or libraries to find examples of Chinese art. Others might eat in a Chinese restaurant and report on the food.

3. Some students might research and report to the rest of the class on Genghis Khan, Kublai Khan, or Marco Polo. Other students might research and report on various forms and examples of Chinese art.

Skills

CHINESE CALLIGRAPHY

Readers' Guide to Periodical Literature

March 1977–February 1978	Abbreviations:

Ap	April
Art N	*Art News*
House B	*House Beautiful*
D	December
il	illustrated
Je	June
Mr	March
N	November
O	October
S	September

Use the above listings from Readers' Guide to Periodical Literature *and information from Chapter 7 to answer the following questions.*

1. How many articles about calligraphy are listed in this edition of *Readers' Guide?*

(a) two (b) five (c) four

2. How many articles which are clearly about Chinese calligraphy are listed?

(a) four (b) one (c) two

3. Which magazine has articles about calligraphy two months in a row?

(a) *House Beautiful* (b) *Seventeen* (c) *Art News*

4. How many of the articles about calligraphy are illustrated?

(a) two (b) three (c) four

5. How does the name of one of these magazines seem to confirm what you learned about calligraphy in Chapter 7?

3
TRADITIONAL LIFE

Chapter 8

Families and Names

THERE NEVER HAS BEEN a "typical Chinese" except in somebody's imagination. And if there had been, that person surely would not have been an emperor, a great philosopher, or any of the others whose names are recorded in the history books.

The most typical Chinese is the farmer. In times past, chances are that he or she belonged to a family which owned or worked a small plot or two. In most periods in Chinese history, farmers and farm families have made up four fifths of China's population.

The crowded river valleys of China are the most farmable areas of the nation. There, settlements march off into the distance, one after another, as far as the eye can see. This has not changed much over the centuries. As an Italian traveler who visited China during the 16th century wrote in his journal: "Of villages and hamlets — the number is infinite; for the country is so covered with habitations that all China seemeth but as one town."

To get an idea of the patterns of life in traditional

China, let's turn back the clock and the calendar. In doing so we should keep in mind that we are talking about a China of the past. Some of the customs and ways of life that will be described still remain. Others do not, because of the many changes that have come to China during the modern era.

If some of the old customs are now out-of-date, why bother talking about them at all? Because we can't begin to understand what China is now changing *into* without first knowing something about what China is changing *from*.

Let's suppose we were to meet a Chinese and discover that her name is Wang Ying-ling.* What can her name alone tell us about China's traditions?

To begin with, her "first name," Wang, is actually her family name (or surname). The Chinese custom of placing the family name first is the opposite of the practice in Western countries.

The rest of our friend Wang's name, Ying-ling, is her given name. Unlike the family names, a person's given name can be almost anything, just as long as the Chinese have a written word for it.

Nor are there given names used especially for boys or girls. Instead the choice of given names is left entirely to the parents (or head of household) who has the honor of bestowing the name on a baby.

Many Chinese have single (one word) given names. But as in the case of Ying-ling, the more common practice is to use a two-word given name. In many families too, all children of the same generation — brothers, sisters, or cousins — share the same "middle name." Wang Ying-ling's older brother, for example, might be named Wang Ying-li,* or her younger brother might be named Wang Ying-ma.* Only the variation in the third part of their names gives each of them his or her individual identity.

Chapter 9

The Traditional Family

THE ORDER in which Chinese names are put together tells us something of how traditional Chinese society was put together. The reason the family name comes first is because the family — not the individual — was the most important unit in the Chinese social order.

An individual's first and foremost responsibility was to his or her own family. The individual was less concerned with finding personal happiness than with the survival and welfare of the family as a whole.

In return the family provided a sense of protection, security, and fellowship. Disputes with outsiders, for example, were usually settled on a family-to-family basis rather than between individuals of different families. When problems arose, members of a family were expected to help those poor members who were in need.

When a Chinese thought of his family, he naturally thought first of the close, or immediate family: a

> **ᴥ§ The individual was less concerned with finding personal happiness than with the welfare of the family as a whole.**

husband, a wife, and their unmarried children all living as one household. This is the basic family unit found in virtually all societies.

But there was another family grouping: the *joint* family. This larger family unit took in the parents, the unmarried children — plus the married children and *their* families. So a joint family usually took in at least three generations, and the eldest pair of parents were actually grandparents. It was a joint family because all its members conducted their family affairs as a single household.

According to the ideals of Old China, all members of a joint family should live under one roof. Rich families, for example, might build a sprawling home with many apartments, all connected with one another by gates and courtyards. But most Chinese families were too poor for mansion-style living. Especially in rural villages, different branches of the joint family lived in separate one-or-two-room cottages, usually within easy walking distance of one another.

Beyond the joint family there were still larger groupings. The most important of these was the clan, which took in everyone who claimed descent from common ancestors. Some clans branched out in many directions. Individual family branches within the clan might live in different villages far apart and achieve different levels of wealth and success. In other cases, especially in South China, members of a clan stuck together so closely that they often created entire villages of their own. In those places, everyone in the

祭神
一年農事遂民庶皆安逸歌謠
遍社村共享昇平世五風雨德
生十兩蒼天濟當年后稷神留
與後人祭

欽天監充官監察司品
鴻臚寺序班臣秦　恭繪

*A Chinese family is shown at the family shrine,
giving thanks to its ancestors for a successful
harvest. Print is from book published in 1696.*

village had the same surname because they were all members of the same clan.

Even death did not end a family relationship. Every Chinese household, no matter how wealthy or humble, had a family shrine somewhere in the home. Wealthy clans sometimes built a separate family temple. In these places, the names of past forebears were recorded on tablets or strips of wood. And at various times of the year, the living family members performed ceremonies to honor their departed ancestors. This reverence for ancestors — some called it "ancestor worship" — gave the family its sense of continuity with the past.

Early in life, each member of the family learned his or her exact role within the family and what duties were expected. These responsibilities were handed down from ancient customs.

The order of importance in a family was quite simple. There were only two basic rules to remember:

1. Age was favored over youth. In the traditional Chinese way of thinking, honor, prestige, and status accumulated with the passing years.

2. Men were favored over women. A wife, for example, was always subordinate to her husband. But for women as well as men, status increased with age.

So the oldest male member ruled the traditional Chinese household. His decisions were the laws of the family. All other members respected his judgment and accepted his decisions.

Or, at least, that was the way it was supposed to look from outside the family. Within the walls of the home, the oldest female member usually had quite a few things to say about how the household was ruled.

Nevertheless, the line of succession in traditional Chinese families was entirely through male heirs. That is to say, when a father died, the oldest son ordinarily became the head of household. This helped to account for the great importance that Chinese families attached to having sons "to carry on the family name." The birth of a son was always an occasion for great rejoicing.

Daughters probably had the worst deal in the old-fashioned Chinese family system. Often a daughter was regarded as hardly more than a "temporary" member of the family. She was usually married off at about the age of 16 and left her own family to move in with her new family. In the process, of course, she gave up her own family name and took the surname of her new family.

Under the old system, even marriages were regarded as something that served the interests of the family rather than of individuals — including those individuals being married. Parents usually arranged the marriages of their children. Usually a third party (either a marriage broker or a friend) served as a go-between to negotiate a proper dowry (gift) from the bride's family or to pick a "lucky day" for the wedding. For a wedding was not so much a time when a man took a wife as a time when the family acquired a daughter-in-law.

Families valued daughters-in-law as potential mothers of sons to carry on the family name. Until the day of motherhood, however, the young wife had little status in her new family. As it frequently worked out, she came completely under the thumb of her mother-in-law. But bearing a son could greatly improve her position with her new relatives.

A wife who failed to bear children (especially a son) could be divorced by her husband. But divorces have always been very unusual in China. Instead old customs made it legal for a husband to take a "secondary wife," called a concubine. Though the con-

cubine did not have the social status of the first or "official wife," children born to the "secondary wife" were treated like all the other children in the family.

In actual practice, though, supporting two (or more) wives was as expensive in China as it was anywhere else. So only the well-to-do or powerful could afford to take on concubines.

To keep everybody squared away on who was who, titles of relationships in a Chinese family were numerous. For example, the title of older brothers (or sisters) differed from the term for younger brothers (or sisters). While parents and elders might call their youngers by endearing nicknames, a younger person wouldn't dream of addressing an older person by, say,

This old print by an unknown artist is called "The Family Visit." If you look at it closely, you'll find that it tells you a great deal about traditional Chinese family life. What does it tell you, for example, about the closeness and size of Chinese families? About the role of women? About the role of old people?

his given name. (That would be shockingly disrespectful!) A common practice was for everyone in the family to call everyone else by their titles of relationship ("father," "mother," "older brother," "younger sister," "third brother"). That made it almost impossible for anyone to forget his or her exact place within the family organization.

Double-check

Review

1. Why is it useful to learn about old Chinese customs even though they are out-of-date?

2. In Chinese names, what comes first — the family name or the given name? What is the reason for the order?

3. What is the principal difference between a basic family unit and a joint family?

4. What two basic rules governed the order of importance of family members in traditional China?

5. What were family members constantly reminded of by the common practice of using titles of relationships?

Discussion

1. As this chapter points out, in old China, individuals were less concerned with finding personal happiness than with the survival and welfare of their families. What effects do you think this had on China's social and political history? What advantages could such a tradition bring to a nation? What disadvantages?

2. Would charges of sexism and ageism have had any meaning in traditional China? What do you think it was like to be a young woman? An old woman?

3. Do you think there was much romantic love in old China? Did there need to be? Why do you suppose divorces have always been rare in China?

Activities

1. Some students might research and report on the order in which names are put together — and its significance — in several other cultures.

2. Several students might role-play this scene: A modern-day Chinese young man brings home his intended bride to introduce her to his family. His grandparents hold strongly traditional ideas; his parents are less traditional, but are surprised that he chose a bride without consulting them. The young woman is intelligent and outspoken, but polite to elders. What happens?

3. A knowledgeable person might be invited to speak to the class about the status of women in traditional and/or modern-day China. If a speaker cannot be found, interested students might do research and report on the subject to the rest of the class.

Skills

IN THE TRADITIONAL FAMILY

The affection between father and son and between husband and wife is natural. How can a law be considered wise when it operates in opposition to this natural affection? Let it be known that from now on a son does not commit a crime if he attempts to conceal the crime of either parent. A wife does not commit a crime if she attempts to conceal the crime of her husband.

— Emperor Hsuan Ti (73-48 B.C.)

Use the passage above and information in Chapters 8 and 9 to answer the following questions.

1. From the information given, what was the author of this passage?
(a) a lawyer   (b) a ruler of China   (c) a husband

2. When did the author of this passage live?
(a) 500 years ago   (b) 48 years ago   (c) 2,000 years ago

3. What are the two main topics of this passage?
(a) fathers and sons   (b) husbands and wives   (c) families and crime

4. The emperor bases his last two statements on what he says is
(a) crime.   (b) natural.   (c) truth.

5. What information in Chapter 9 does the emperor's ruling emphasize?

Chapter 10

Close to the Land

THE FAMILY was not only the basic social unit of traditional China. It was also the basic economic unit. Aside from an individual's own personal belongings, all wealth and property were owned jointly by the family members. Similarly the family income was shared by all members.

And when people in old China thought about wealth, the first thing that came to mind was land. In the river valleys and wide plains of China's most fertile region, there never seemed to be enough land to go around. So land ownership became a mark by which to measure the success or failure of a family.

For most Chinese families, land was especially important. Land not only served as the family's main source of livelihood. It was also the burial place of the family's ancestors. Thus, loss of this land was not only an economic blow but also a spiritual disaster to the family.

The pattern of land use in the Chinese countryside was very different from that found in the U.S. In the

U.S., a single farm might sprawl over hundreds of acres, with an isolated farmhouse on it. The nearest neighbor might be quite a way down the road.

In the crowded Chinese countryside, no one lived in isolation. Farm families clustered their houses together in villages and hamlets, both for protection and to save space.

The land worked by an individual Chinese farm family was very small. Moreover, the family land usually didn't come as one solid chunk. Instead a family might own a strip of land here, a wedge over there, and rent a third piece farther away — all unconnected with one another and far apart.

The Chinese farmer reasoned that the quality of soil differed from one place to the next. Now if one farmer owned a solid chunk of land in one place, he might get all the best soil while everyone else got stuck with bad soil. By taking little pieces here and there, each farmer stood a better chance of getting at least some good soil. The main problem with this setup was that farmers wasted a lot of time getting from home out to the field and then from one field to another.

The scarcity of good farmland in China made it uneconomic for large plots to be left for grazing or pasturing. For that reason, huge herds of cattle or sheep were unknown to the vast majority of Chinese. Farm families might raise a few hogs, goats, or chickens. And if a family was fairly well off, it might also own a water buffalo or an ox. But these last two were used as work animals and not raised for food.

Instead most of the fertile land was given over to the growing of grains. Except in the wheat-growing areas of the north, that meant rice growing. Smaller patches of land might also be used for growing vegetables of various kinds.

ᐭ **A family might own a strip of land here, a wedge over there, and rent a third piece—all unconnected with one another.**

Chinese farming methods remained unchanged for many centuries. Rice growing required large amounts of water. This, in turn, meant that fields had to be leveled and terraced, mud embankments had to be built to keep the water in, and irrigation canals had to be kept in constant repair. Water was moved from plot to plot by use of simple machinery, usually powered by human muscles.

Each spring the soil was broken up, a task done with either a wooden plow drawn by a water buffalo or by pulling by hand a sort of forked hoe through the flooded rice paddy. After that the seeds were sown in the flooded field. When the young seedlings reached about six inches high, each stalk was pulled up by hand, one stalk at a time. They were then transplanted into a larger flooded field by hand, one by one.

From time to time throughout the growing season, the paddies were drained, weeded, and then reflooded. Finally the rice plants ripened and the fields were drained for the last time. Farmers using hand sickles went into the field to cut and bundle the rice stalks.

But even then their work wasn't finished. The rice grains had to be separated from the stalks, by hand, either by whacking the stalks against something or whacking the stalks with pitchforks. Next the grains were pounded, by hand, in a mortar to separate the

Strips and wedges of farmland fill the landscape.

Shin-deep in water and mud, Chinese farmers plow their rice fields and sow their seed. This is how Chinese farmers worked thousands of years ago. Many still do it the same way today.

husks. Then the rice had to be winnowed, by hand, to sift out the husks from the grain. The finished rice was collected in baskets and put away in storage for use through the next year. And only then could the farmers stop to rest their weary bodies.

Because of the awesome amount of human labor that went into rice growing in China, each male member of the family was expected to pitch in with the field work. Only the very old and the very young were excused. When a Chinese peasant child reached the age of six or seven, the days of fun and games were pretty much over. At the beginning he or she was given only the simplest and lightest tasks. But the jobs got tougher as the youth grew older, bigger, and stronger.

During the busy planting or harvesting times, women often went out to the fields to lend a hand. But most of the time women worked around the home doing all those endless household chores: washing, sewing, and cooking.

Since rice was the main food crop, it followed that rice was also the staple food of the Chinese. Rice in some form usually appeared at every meal (indeed, the Chinese phrase for "meal" is literally "eat rice"). But unless times were bad, the Chinese family would not sit down to a meal of only rice and nothing else. A few vegetable dishes were provided to give the meal some flavor. Less often perhaps, some meat or fish dish might also be added to the menu.

Hopefully the farm family had grown enough food to feed itself and meet the tax and rent bills as well. Or if the crop had been especially good, the family might have some food left over to sell in a nearby town. Often farm families supplemented their income during the slack season by working at basket making, cloth weaving, or some other kind of handicraft. The money earned was used to buy seeds for next year's planting or goods that the family needed. And, if the family had a few good years, there might be enough money saved up to buy or rent another plot of land.

But floods, drought, wars, or other disasters could bring crop failure, hunger, debt, and very often loss of land. For the great masses of Chinese peasants, life was never easy.

☆　☆　☆　☆　☆　☆　☆　☆　☆

The Chinese farmer spent the better part of his life doing hard, back-breaking work. For most farmers the endless routine of work was broken up only by

It's off to market for this fortunate peasant husband and wife and their unfortunate pig.

the festivals and celebrations sprinkled all through the calendar year.

Specific holidays differed from place to place according to local customs. But hardly a month went by anywhere in China when there wasn't a celebration of some sort. Most of the holidays honored legendary gods and heroes or the spirits of departed ancestors.

The most colorful ceremony during the summer was the Dragon Boat Festival. This honored a statesman-poet of ancient times, Ch'u Yuan,* who was said to have been falsely accused of disloyalty to his em-

94

peror. Legend had it that this discouraged statesman then flung himself into a river. The people, however, knew of his goodness, and they jumped into boats and paddled furiously to try to save him. Alas, they didn't get to the drowning man in time. They could only scatter some rice, wrapped in bamboo leaves, to comfort his spirit. After that, the fifth day of the fifth month was marked each year by dragon boat races on the river and the eating of rice dumplings wrapped in bamboo leaves.

By far the most important and merriest holiday came at the beginning of each year — the Chinese New Year. This came on the first day of the year according to the ancient lunar calendar of China. It usually fell sometime in late January or early February in the modern calendar.

Actually preparation and related festivals started 15 days before the new year and kept going for 15 days after the new year. By the middle of the 12th month, the family closed out the business activities for the year and repaid all debts so as to start the next year with a clean slate. On the 23rd day of that month, the family Kitchen God received special homage. For many believed that the Kitchen God was about to make his annual trip to heaven to report on the conduct of the family during the past year. Food, wine, and money were offered to the Kitchen God to put him in a better mood for a favorable accounting. The entire house was thoroughly cleaned to await the Kitchen God's return on New Year's Eve.

The main object of the celebration was to insure good fortune through the coming year. Firecrackers were set off to scare away evil spirits, and red paper scrolls were tacked up around the house to bring good luck. Ancestors were honored with elaborate ritual.

But it was also a time for fun. The fanciest feast of

95

the year came on New Year's Day. Young people received gifts from their parents and elders. The family put on new clothes to visit relatives and friends, offering congratulations all around and wishes for future prosperity.

☆   ☆   ☆   ☆   ☆   ☆   ☆   ☆   ☆

For the peasants of China, family and village comprised almost the entire world. Most Chinese farmers tended to regard the government as something that came around to collect taxes or draft their sons into armies. Their fondest wish was to be left alone by "outsiders" so that they could work out their own problems.

Sometimes, though, outside forces made the life of the Chinese peasantry unbearable. Chinese history is filled with examples of peasant revolts. But these revolts were usually aimed at a change of rulers — *not* the system. For after each change of rulers, the peasants went back to doing the same things in the same old ways they'd always been done.

Shimmering in the early morning light, the Forbidden City of the Ming emperors is a monument of great beauty and power.

THE "BRILLIANT" AND "PURE" DYNASTIES

OF ALL THE REBEL LEADERS who fought to oust the Mongols from China in the 14th century, the most successful was Chu Yuan-chang.* He was a man of humble birth who had received only a smattering of education. But Chu was a man of great military ability. After the Mongol hold was broken, he named himself the first emperor in the new ruling line of the Ming* (meaning "brilliant") dynasty. His rule was extremely harsh. But he firmly established the foundations of a dynasty that would hold China's throne for nearly 300 years, from 1368 to 1644.

The beginning of the new dynasty saw a burst of national vigor. The early Ming emperors worked to restore China to past glories. Classical scholarship was once more held in high esteem. The examination system was revived as a way of selecting scholar-officials for the civil service. There was a renewed interest in China's literature and arts.

Under the Ming, the capital of the Chinese empire was moved to Peking, which was rebuilt to include a new and magnificent Imperial City. At the center of the Imperial City was the residence of the emperor himself — the "Forbidden City" — a complex of palaces and courtyards that is still admired as one of China's greatest architectural gems.

It was under the Ming dynasty that China reached its peak as a sea power. Large fleets of Chinese junks explored much of Southeast Asia and crossed the Bay of Bengal to Ceylon and India. Later voyages took Chinese seafarers across the Indian Ocean to the Persian Gulf, Red Sea, and the east coast of Africa.

But at the end of the 15th century, the seagoing traffic started moving in the opposite direction. Europeans had launched their own Age of Exploration. In 1498 the Portuguese navigator Vasco da Gama rounded the southern tip of Africa to become the first European to reach India by sea. Other Portuguese seafarers reached China in 1514. And in 1557 they established the first European settlement in China at Macao,* near the city of Canton.

Most of the early European seagoing adventurers were attracted by the fabled riches of the East, which they hoped to tap through trade or plunder. A smaller group, however, went for a different purpose. They were Jesuit missionaries who hoped to convert the Chinese empire to Christianity.

To better perform their mission, many of the Jesuits in China turned themselves into respected Chinese scholars, mastering the Chinese language. (Thus while they were still regarded by the Chinese as foreigners, they were certainly not "barbarians.")

Just about the time the Europeans began entering China, the power of the Ming dynasty began to fade. A people to the north called the Manchus were becoming increasingly powerful. Then, while the Mings were wracked by a power struggle at the top, the Manchus marched into North China. They captured Peking in 1644 and formed a new ruling dynasty, for which they chose the name Ch'ing* (or "pure").

For the second time in its history, all China came under the rule of foreigners. But the Manchus found themselves with a problem: They ruled over a people who outnumbered them by at least 50 to one. They feared they might in time be overwhelmed by the Chinese majority all around them.

To prevent this, the Manchus set up a system designed to keep themselves and the Chinese apart. Manchus and Chinese were not allowed to intermarry. The Chinese were not allowed to settle in Manchuria. In China itself, Manchu military garrisons were housed in walled-off compounds separated from the Chinese people. And the Manchus forced all adult male Chinese to wear their hair in a long, single pigtail — called a queue* — as a sign of submission to the Manchu emperor.

The Manchu rulers brought a period of peace and stability to China which lasted about 150 years. Manchu armies extended the boundaries of the empire to include an area unmatched since Han times. Many smaller Asian states — Korea, Annam (the northern part of Vietnam), Burma, Thailand, and Nepal became "vassals" of the Manchu-Chinese "celestial empire."

But even as the Manchu rulers gloried in their achievements, the seeds of their destruction were being sown. The new challenge came from people who were even more foreign to China than the Manchus. These "more foreign foreigners" were the Europeans.

Double-check

Review

1. Why did most Chinese farmers work several small plots of land rather than one large plot?

2. In the Chinese language, what is the literal meaning of the phrase for "meal"?

3. What was the most important holiday in China?

4. Where is the Forbidden City? Whose residence was it?

5. What was the origin of the Chinese pigtail, or queue?

Discussion

1. How do traditional Chinese attitudes about land compare to the attitudes of early American Indians? Early white settlers in America? Present-day land use in the United States? What is the evidence for your answers?

2. Do you think holidays were more important in traditional China than they are now? Why, or why not? In what ways was the celebration of the traditional Chinese New Year similar to the celebration of New Year's Eve in the United States? How was it different?

3. Can you describe any modern parallels to the ways in which the Manchus kept control of the Chinese and kept themselves separate from the Chinese? Explain your answer.

Activities

1. The entire class might role-play a meeting of the people of a small Chinese village trying to decide if they should end the traditional pattern of scattered land use and trade plots so that each family can farm one plot rather than several tiny plots. What changes would be necessary? How could plots, burial grounds, crops, water rights, etc., be exchanged fairly? Try to work out a plan.

2. Some students might prepare a bulletin board display on traditional and modern Chinese celebrations of holidays.

3. Some students might research and report on developments during the Ming dynasty, especially Chinese exploration of other lands by sea and the eventual influx of Europeans to China. Information gathered could be marked on a large wall map, showing routes of exploration, spheres of influence, etc.

Skills

LAND USE IN CHINA

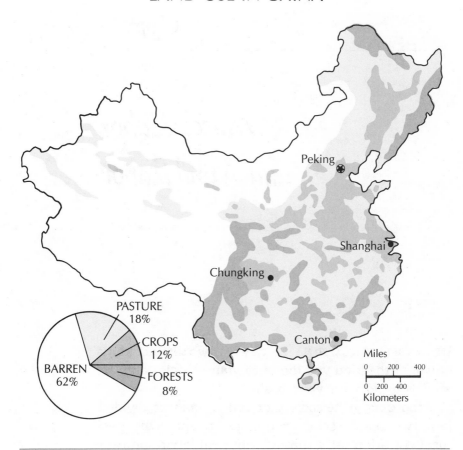

Use the map and circle graph above and information in Chapter 10 to answer the following questions.

1. How much of China is covered with forests?

2. Crops and pasture together cover how much land?

3. Most of the barren land is in what part of China?

4. About how many miles west of the capital of China does the barren land begin?

5. What information in Chapter 10 about rice combines with this map to enable you to figure out the general location of most of China's rivers?

Chapter 11

Muscle Labor and Mind Labor

IN TRADITIONAL CHINA, there were two distinct kinds of work: the kind you did with your muscles and the kind you did with your brain.

Accordingly the society of Old China was divided into two main social groupings: people who performed work mostly through physical labor and people who worked mostly with their minds.

The first group, sometimes termed "body-laborers," were the "common people." Tradition further divided this group into three occupational classes: peasants, craftsmen, and merchants. (Actually the class lines were not so neatly drawn. A farmer, for example, might also work as a spare-time craftsman and, hence, be a member of two occupational classes at the same time.)

The other — and much smaller — social group consisted of the gentry. What set the gentry apart from

Can you write a caption for this old print based on your reading of the chapter? What are the men in the center doing? The men at the bottom?

◄§ Some scholars let their fingernails grow to great lengths. Many developed a slightly bent-over posture, admired as a "scholar's stoop."

---

the commoner was that the gentry had little need to exert any physical labor in order to earn a living. If a gentry family owned land, the members of this family would not farm it themselves. Instead the land would be worked by hired hands or would be rented out to farmers.

Since the gentry didn't work their own land, there was no reason why they had to live in the villages. Many gentry families became absentee landlords, preferring to live in towns and cities some distance away from the family property. They were attracted to the towns and cities for a number of reasons: for example, the excitement and convenience of life in towns and cities and the greater cultural and economic opportunities there.

The gentry were not only the leisure class but also the educated class. The two, in fact, went hand in hand. A scholar was one who had mastered the language, classical literature, and the arts. Because this involved many years of difficult training, the would-be scholar began his studies early in life. From age four on, he started to build up a written vocabulary, learning how to write the complicated Chinese characters with the proper strokes and committing the words to memory.

From that he moved on to the books of Chinese classical literature, memorizing whole texts. After years at this, a diligent student could recite whole books by memory, word for word. Only then was he allowed to study the learned notes and comments of famous scholars to help him understand what he had been reciting during all those previous years.

Schooling was a no-nonsense affair. Teachers or tutors walked around with bamboo canes in hand to make sure the students paid attention to their lessons. Would-be scholars soon learned to devote almost all waking hours to "mind labor" and to shun anything that suggested physical work.

Such gentle pastimes as painting, composing poetry, bird watching, and sitting quietly by a riverbank with a fishing pole were thought to be acceptable for the educated gentleman. But running, swimming, or other vigorous activities were considered undignified. Some scholars let their fingernails grow to great lengths as a sign that they never had to do any manual labor. Many also developed a slightly bent-over posture, widely admired as a "scholar's stoop."

To some the life of a scholar-gentry might not sound like much fun. Yet it was a style of life that all Chinese, rich or poor, dreamed of attaining, though relatively few actually did so. "Mind labor" was surely more agreeable work — or, at least, a lot less tiring and tedious — than "body labor." A high level of education brought great prestige to the scholar and his family and opened doors to opportunity. For the scholar-gentry formed the ruling class in traditional China. As was written in the *Book of Mencius*:

"Those who labor with their minds govern; those who labor with their strength are governed. Those who are governed serve; those who govern are served. This is a principle universally recognized."

Chapter 12

The Celestial Empire

THE SOLE RULER of the traditional Chinese world was the emperor. He alone was thought to possess the "Mandate of Heaven," which would enable him to maintain harmony on earth. He was, indeed, looked upon by his subjects as the connection between the world of mankind and the immense universe.

The emperor was all-powerful. He had no equal. Still he was only one man, and his domain was vast. He couldn't be everywhere at once or know everything that was going on. As a rule, Chinese emperors didn't care very much for travel, and many never ventured out of their own capital.

So the direct authority of the emperor did not usually bear down too heavily on the day-to-day lives of the people. Most of the daily affairs of the people were taken care of by the family, the village council, or craft guilds.

"Exam Day" for candidates for government
office in old China. Was the Chinese way of
selecting government officials a fair one?

ᴥ§ Each official had to take care that his career was not cut short. A minor misdeed might bring instant dismissal; a major one could lead to exile or death.

To bridge the gap between the authority of the central government and the units of local rule, a huge civil service was created. And this was where the scholar-official came into the picture.

The idea of rule by scholars began as early as Han times and was further developed over the years. These officials were to be selected on their merit and not because of high birth or family connections.

"Merit" in this case meant a thorough knowledge of the Confucian classics. Candidates for government jobs were tested in official examinations held regularly throughout the empire. Those who successfully passed the examinations were given degrees. Those who failed (and, usually, more failed than passed) were allowed to take the exams over and over again until they eventually passed — or gave up. Those who passed the first examination could go on to a series of more difficult examinations leading to higher and higher degrees.

A degree holder was an officially recognized "scholar" and, therefore, eligible for appointment to the imperial civil service. The rules said that an official could not serve in his home district or province (lest he be tempted to bestow special favors on his family and friends). More often than not, the official found himself dispatched to some distant post half way across the empire. Nor was he allowed to stay in one job for more than a few years. Thus the official spent a large part of his career moving from one post to another. At the same time each official had to take care that his career was not cut short. A minor misdeed in office might bring instant dismissal; a major one could lead to exile in some remote corner of the empire, or even death.

Despite the risks, government appointments were eagerly sought. There were always more degree holders than there were jobs available. The competition was intense. Most of the scholar-officials came from the gentry class, since this was the educated class to begin with. But the public examinations were open to all classes. And there were many instances of bright lads from humble circumstances who succeeded in passing the examinations and winning the coveted official appointments. (In the process, of course, they elevated themselves and their families out of their "humble circumstances" right into the privileged gentry class.)

The scholar-gentry provided the old Chinese world with a highly cultured corps of leaders and officials. But since they were all cast from the same educational mold, they all tended to think very much alike and to value the same things. They emphasized classical learning to the virtual exclusion of such "practical arts" as engineering, commerce, or military science. They were far more interested in keeping things as they were than in promoting reforms — for changes might threaten their positions of privilege in the system.

Double-check

Review

1. What were the two main social groups in traditional China?

2. Why did some Chinese scholars let their fingernails grow to great lengths?

3. Who was the sole ruler of the ancient Chinese world? What was he expected to do with his "Mandate of Heaven"?

4. Why was a huge civil service system created in China?

5. Why weren't civil service officials allowed to serve in their home districts or provinces?

Discussion

1. Is the division of work into two distinct kinds — muscle labor and mind labor — unrealistic? Why, or why not? Did it make sense in traditional China? Was it a natural outgrowth of other Chinese traditions? Explain.

2. How "democratic" was ancient China's civil service system? Do you think rule by scholars is a good idea? Was it a good idea for ancient China? Why, or why not? What kinds of things should rulers know?

3. Was it a good idea in ancient China to send government officials away from their home provinces? What strong Chinese tradition might have made this necessary? How would you argue against such a system?

Activities

1. One student might play the role of a U.S. union leader transported back into ancient China. She or he could try to convince three skeptical Chinese laborers (fellow students) to organize and demand better training and higher wages.

2. Two small groups of students might take opposite sides for an informal debate of the following statement: Resolved, that it is natural and good that "those who labor with their minds govern; those who labor with their strength are governed. Those who are governed serve; those who govern are served."

3. Some students might research and report to the rest of the class on other cultures' ideas about the relation between mind and body, especially those of ancient Greece.

Skills

TWO MEASURES OF EDUCATION
IN FIVE COUNTRIES

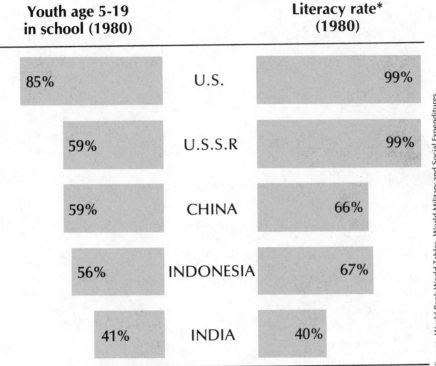

Youth age 5-19 in school (1980)		Literacy rate* (1980)
85%	U.S.	99%
59%	U.S.S.R	99%
59%	CHINA	66%
56%	INDONESIA	67%
41%	INDIA	40%

*Citizens aged 15 and above who can read and write.

Source: World Bank World Tables, World Military and Social Expenditures

Use the bar graph above and information from Chapters 11 and 12 to answer the following questions.

1. The percentages in this graph are for what year?

2. According to this graph, what is the percentage of China's adult population that can read and write?

3. Which country has the highest percentage of children between the ages of five and 19 in school?

4. Are there any figures in this graph that seem unrealistically high? Why might nations inflate some of these statistics?

5. According to this graph, what situation described in Chapter 11 had changed drastically by 1980?

THE
LAND

In a land of many people and rugged terrain, little usable land goes to waste. Left, the terraced rice fields of Yenan run up a mountainside like a giant's staircase. Below, a hospital in Fukien province perches precariously on a riverbank with the Wu I* mountains towering over it.

*VARIETY: From city to countryside, China
presents a vast and varied face. Clockwise
from top: the pagodas of the old section
of Peking, a snowy pass in the Tien Shan
mountains, the Gobi desert's sandy wastes,
and northern China's rich wheat fields.*

THE
PEOPLE

*China's many millions are a complex
of individuals who can't be summed up
in a few pat phrases. But some of
the things that draw most Chinese
together are a sense of pride in
Chinese culture, respect for the
elderly, and a thorough concern for
the maintenance of close family ties.*

MINORITIES: Outsiders often think that all Chinese are alike. But these stereotypes ignore the richness and variety of the Chinese people. The people on these pages are all members of various Chinese ethnic minorities. They are as follows: above, Hui; top right, Mongolian; right, Tibetan.

THE ECONOMY

China's economy has made enormous progress in the past few decades. Power plants, such as the one at left, designed and built by Chinese, are sprouting up across the country. But with all the progress, China's main power source remains human muscle.

122

WORK: *Despite industrialization, most Chinese are not involved in industry, but in tasks such as farming, grazing, and fishing. Left, arid western China is poor farmland, but excellent grazing land; below, northern China is a first-rate area for wheat (here being bagged for market); above, waters off southern China yield a rich harvest of fish.*

MATTER OF DEGREE: Industry in China comes in many shapes and sizes, from large-scale oil drilling in Gobi desert, top left, to "back-yard" industries such as steel-making in villages, left, to small "hand" industries such as making rings for buckets.

柳陰高士写為
高枝浪那臧意
自豪設問伊人
何旺民於唐居
李晉弓旬浩

丁亥畫月浩起

126

THE CULTURE

China today draws cultural sustenance from the rich and proud heritage of its past. Much has been changed by the Communists, but much endures today. Old prints here symbolize scholarly tradition, left, and respect for authority, below. Do these historic traditions exist in China today?

ARTS: Sculpture, pottery making, architecture, painting, and calligraphy — all these and much more are essential parts of the rich cultural legacy of old China. What other arts at which the Chinese excel are described in this book?

ALIVE AND WELL: Whether practicing an ancient system of exercising, learning their rich but difficult language, or enjoying the art of sword dancing, the Chinese know their culture is a living and vital force.

130

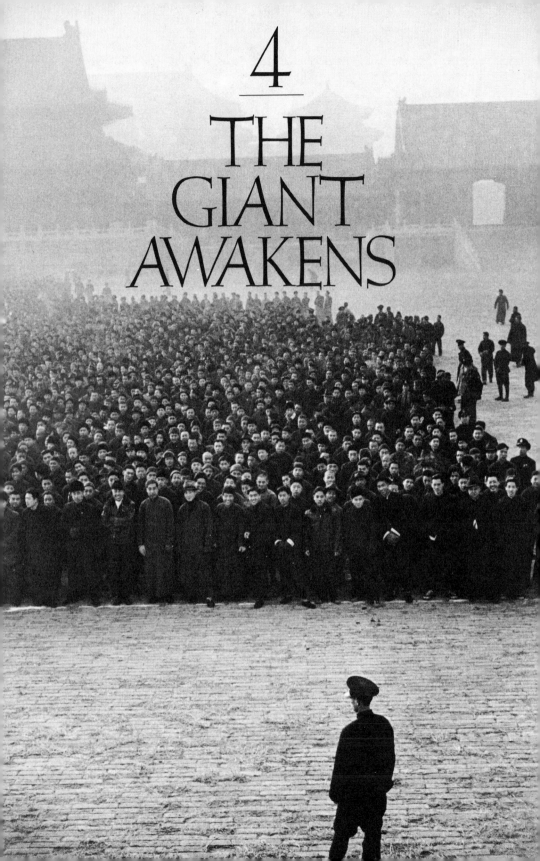

4
THE
GIANT
AWAKENS

Chapter 13

A Century of Humiliation

AT FIRST the influence of Europe on China was so slight that the Chinese hardly noticed. Since the Chinese rulers regarded their nation as the only really civilized region of the world, it was easy for them to assume that Europeans were just so many more "barbarians."

Canton was the only Chinese port opened to the foreign traders. And in Canton the Europeans were required to deal with only a small group of Chinese merchants licensed by the Chinese government. Foreigners were not permitted to travel to any other part of China or to mingle with other Chinese. The foreign traders were required to leave as soon as their business was finished.

Even with these restrictions, a flourishing trade developed for the goods of China — mostly tea, but also porcelain tableware, silk and cotton fabrics, and art and furniture made by skilled Chinese craftsmen from ivory, jade, brass, bronze, and lacquered wood.

Then another item, opium, began to loom large in the China trade. British merchants discovered that opium was a much desired product in China although its import into China was illegal. In time they found that opium-smuggling held out promises of huge profits.

Opium had long been used in China as medicine. Later it was used by some people to help them forget their problems, even though it ruined their health. And as the British smuggled more opium into China, more Chinese began smoking it.

Finally the Chinese government took action to stamp out the opium trade. A special commissioner was sent to Canton to break up the smuggling network. He confined all foreign traders and forced them to surrender some 20,000 chests of opium, which were then publicly burned.

The British government was furious at the Chinese action. A number of incidents flared into a major clash. This was the beginning of a series of conflicts between the British and Chinese, which historians call the Opium War.

From the time of the Opium War in 1839, China's fortunes skidded downhill. Ironically the defenders of the civilization which first invented gunpowder were still fighting with swords and arrows, while the Western "barbarians" had long since passed the Chinese in industrial and military technology. The result was a string of defeats for China.

To end the Opium War, the Manchus were forced to accept stiff terms. The Chinese agreed to open four more ports to foreign trade. They gave the island of Hong Kong, just off the China coast, to Britain. (It remains a British colony to the present day.) And China was forced to pay the British 21 million dollars.

*Foreign trading "factories" in Canton harbor
in the mid-19th century. Can you identify any
of the foreign nations from the flags shown?*

Before the Opium War, the Chinese dealt with foreigners as "superiors" might deal with "inferiors."
Now the roles were reversed. For the next 100 years,
the foreigners dictated the terms, while the Chinese
were powerless to do very much about it.

For China the second half of the 19th century was
a sad rerun of the first — another round of military
defeats, followed by more concessions to the foreign
powers. The Yangtze River was opened to foreign
ships. This opened inland China to foreign influence
and commerce.

All around the edges of China, Europeans nibbled
away at the Chinese empire. Britain ended Chinese
control of Burma and Nepal. France seized Annam

135

and went on to assemble a colony in Indochina. Russia took control of large areas of the northeast. Germany gained a foothold on the Shantung* Peninsula.

Later Japan was added to the list of foreign powers pushing their way into China. Like China, Japan had enjoyed a long period of "splendid isolation." That ended in 1854, when the ships of U.S. Commodore Matthew Perry showed up and pried Japan open to foreign contacts and trade. Unlike China, which resisted change, Japan moved rapidly to convert itself into a modern industrial state.

The first test of Japan's newly developed power was in Korea in 1894. A clash between Chinese and Japanese interests there led to war. Japan's modernized army and navy crushed the Chinese forces. China was forced to withdraw from Korea and to give the island of Taiwan to Japan.

Now China's "century of humiliation" seemed nearly complete. The European powers and Japan were ready to carve up all of China and divide the spoils among themselves. Yet they stopped just short of this final indignity.

Why? Mostly because the foreign powers realized that, if they did this, they might start fighting one another for China's riches. In the end the foreign powers accepted a U.S. proposal called the "Open Door Policy Doctrine." Under it all major powers would have equal rights to trade with China, but not to seize its territory.

For China the 19th century was a time of shock and shame. And as the nation reeled from the assaults of the foreign powers, its social fabric quickly unwound.

For one thing, China's population grew enormously. At the beginning of the 18th century, it

Foreign Powers Nibble at China's Borders (1842-1912)

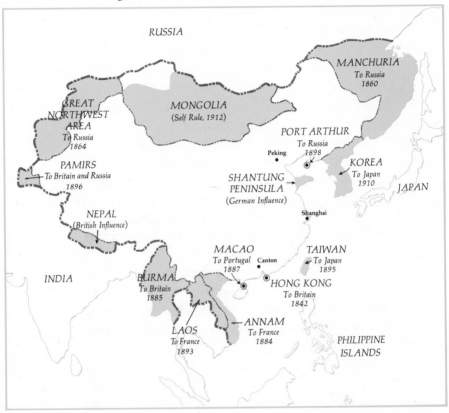

RUSSIA

MANCHURIA
To Russia
1860

GREAT
NORTHWEST
AREA
To Russia
1864

MONGOLIA
(Self Rule, 1912)

PORT ARTHUR
To Russia
1898

Peking

KOREA
To Japan
1910

JAPAN

PAMIRS
To Britain and Russia
1896

SHANTUNG
PENINSULA
(German Influence)

NEPAL
(British Influence)

Shanghai

INDIA

MACAO
To Portugal
1887

Canton

TAIWAN
To Japan
1895

BURMA
To Britain
1885

HONG KONG
To Britain
1842

LAOS
To France
1893

ANNAM
To France
1884

PHILIPPINE
ISLANDS

was about 150 million. By the middle of the 19th century, it had almost tripled — to about 400 million. Food production over the same period did not increase at anywhere near this rate. Add to this the recurrence of floods and droughts. The result: some of the worst famines in China's history.

As usual most of the burden fell on China's peasants. Farmers lost their land or went hopelessly into debt to landlords and money-lenders. Desperate parents abandoned their infants to starvation or sold their children into bondage because they had no way to feed another mouth in the family.

Many of those driven off the land drifted to the

ports where they barely made a living as coolies (manual laborers) or servants, doing any work that might bring in a few cents a day. Soon many of China's large cities became ugly, overcrowded, festering slums.

It was a time ripe for revolts, which broke out by the dozens. Of these the Boxer Uprising of 1900 was to leave the deepest scars on a strife-torn land.

The secret society which led the rebellion went under the name of "Righteousness and Harmony." But because of a translation mix-up and because its members practiced a traditional form of Chinese exercises that resembled shadow boxing, Westerners came to call the group "Boxers."

The Boxers were fanatically antiforeign. They practiced magic rites in the belief that this would protect them from the gunfire of the foreign troops. Breaking out of their strongholds in the north, roving bands of Boxers killed hundreds of foreign missionaries and Chinese Christian converts.

With official support from the ruling Manchu imperial court, the Boxers were admitted to Peking. Here they murdered the German government's representative and trapped all foreign residents in the section of the city in which the foreign diplomats lived. And, almost as an afterthought, the Chinese government declared war on all foreign powers.

Stunned governments in distant parts of the world hastily assembled an international army which fought its way into Peking and managed to rescue the foreigners who had been trapped for eight weeks, fighting for their lives. Though the Boxer Uprising and other rebellions failed, they were clear signs of mounting anger and frustration in China.

The Manchu rulers simply could not cope with the demands of rapidly changing times. A living symbol

A 1902 photograph shows some of the officers in the foreign occupation army sent to China to quell the Boxer uprising. Can you identify the nationality of any of these officers?

of the corruption of the Manchus in its last 50 years was the Empress Dowager Tzu Hsi.* She was a strong-willed woman who held the real power of the government by ruling as regent for a series of weak or child emperors. As an example of her ruling style, she once took tax money intended for building a modern Chinese navy and used it instead to build a summer palace with a large marble boat sitting in the lake — unmoving and entirely useless for the defense of China.

The old empress died in 1908. Four years later, the last imperial dynasty to rule over China broke up and sank out of sight.

Double-check

Review

1. List three ways in which the rulers of 19th-century China tried to restrict trade and contact with foreigners.

2. Name three of the principal trade goods Europeans wanted from China.

3. Name four of the nations which took control of Chinese territory during the 19th century.

4. What was the "Open Door Doctrine"?

5. In what year did the last imperial dynasty to rule China break up?

Discussion

1. What did British traders' smuggling of opium into China suggest about British attitudes toward the Chinese? Why might this be called "ironical"? What could a government do to another nation it knew was smuggling illegal drugs into the country?

2. When European powers began moving into China, Napoleon Bonaparte said: "China? There lies a sleeping giant. Let him sleep, for when he wakes he will move the world." What facts about China might have led Bonaparte to make this statement at that time?

3. Should China have allowed foreign traders into Canton? Once they did, was it simply a matter of time before more encroachments came? Can isolation be a good — or realistic — stance for a nation? Explain your answers.

Activities

1. Some students might research and report to the rest of the class on the Boxer Uprising of 1900.

2. The entire class might pretend that it is a meeting of Chinese elders discussing whether or not to allow the first European traders to come into Canton. Some might argue for keeping the "barbarians" out of China completely. Others might advocate moderate trade. And still others could argue for completely accepting European trade and cultural influence. After the discussion, take a vote.

3. Some students might pretend they are the Empress Dowager Tzu Hsi. Write her last entry in her diary as she sits in her summer palace thinking about what will happen to China when she dies.

Skills

Use information and the map, "Foreign Powers Nibble at China's Borders (1842-1912)," in Chapter 13 to answer the questions below. On a separate sheet of paper, write the number of each question. Then write the letter of the best answer next to the number of each question.

Answers

(a) **Hong Kong**

(b) **Korea**

(c) **Shantung Peninsula**

(d) **Mongolia**

(e) **North**

(f) **South**

(g) **Russia**

(h) **India**

(i) **Taiwan**

1. In what part of China was most of the territory that was taken over by Russia?

2. What territory was under German influence during this period?

3. What island was taken over by Japan in 1895?

4. What territory was taken over by Japan in 1910 and then later became two separate countries?

5. What country took away the most territory from China during this period?

6. Which territory achieved independence from China at about the same time that the last imperial Chinese dynasty broke up?

Chapter 14

Father of Modern China

CHINA, almost a world unto itself since the beginning of history, could hardly manage its own affairs at the start of the 20th century. Foreign powers had assumed a commanding role over China's political and commercial affairs. Foreign officials ran China's maritime customs and national postal services. Most of its new factories, railroads, telegraph, and shipping lines were foreign-financed and foreign-controlled. Gunboats flying foreign flags cruised China's rivers to enforce the foreigners' privileges and to protect foreign nationals and investments.

The Chinese were bewildered and resentful. New generations of Chinese thinkers were forced to face up to some difficult questions: Why couldn't China resist the challenge of Western imperialism? What made the foreign powers so strong? How could China come to terms with the forces of a modern world?

For the first time a steady trickle of young Chinese

began going abroad to study in foreign lands. From these returning students, and from the presence of Westerners in China, the ideas of Western science, philosophy, and government began to spread in China.

This brought growing pressures for change in China. Despite widespread unrest, however, China's Manchu rulers were neither willing nor able to make reforms.

Yet events would not wait for the Manchus. In 1911 a revolution began in China that swept away not only the Manchu regime but some of China's old traditions as well.

To cut through the twists and turns of the development of 20th-century China, we will follow the careers of three men who have dominated its course: Sun Yat-sen,* Chiang Kai-shek,* and Mao Tse-tung.*

☆ ☆ ☆ ☆ ☆ ☆ ☆ ☆ ☆

"I am a coolie," he once described himself. But in the tradition of Confucius 2,500 years before, Sun Yat-sen gave himself a more humble background than was actually the case. His father worked for a time as a tailor, later as a small trader, and finally settled down to farm a small piece of family-owned land near Canton.

Here Sun was born in 1866, in the region of China which had the longest history of foreign contact. Many families in the Canton region had sons or relatives who had gone abroad to seek their fortunes. When Sun was 13, he was sent to Honolulu to be educated, joining an elder brother who had immigrated there earlier. By the time Sun returned home at the age of 17, he was already in rebellion against the old Chinese ways.

Sun Yat-sen: "Father of Modern-Day China."

A year later, Sun went to British-ruled Hong Kong to become a medical doctor. Although he was more interested in developing a revolutionary philosophy, Sun realized that the title of "Dr." in front of his name would help to give him, in his own words, "free access everywhere."

After his return from Hong Kong, he organized a secret society whose aim was to overthrow China's Manchu dynasty and establish a republic. But his first real attempt at revolutionary action fizzled disastrously. Many of the plotters were rounded up and executed by the authorities. Sun himself just managed to escape to Japan.

Sun traveled about the world drumming up support and raising funds. His activities alarmed the Manchu government. Once, while he was in England, Sun was kidnapped and held prisoner in the Chinese legation in London. Facing a one-way trip home to certain death, Sun managed to smuggle out a note telling of his plight. The British people were outraged at the kidnapping, and the Chinese were forced to release Sun unharmed.

For 15 years, Sun traveled around the world, organizing support for his cause. Then one day in 1911 while traveling in the U.S., he received electrifying news: A major revolt had exploded in China.

It was almost a revolution by accident. In an investigation of a bomb blast in Hankow,* the Manchu police had stumbled onto a secret revolutionary headquarters and bomb factory. In the rubble they had found a membership list of the local revolutionaries which, interestingly enough, contained the names of quite a few young officers in a nearby army garrison.

Their conspiracy discovered, the rebels rose and, to their own astonishment, seized three cities with hardly a struggle.

The sudden uprising touched off a chain reaction of revolts. One after the other, the southern provinces declared themselves against the Manchu government. Even though its imperial army was a powerful force in the north, the Manchu regime was clearly moving toward a final collapse.

A triumphant Sun Yat-sen returned to China to a hero's welcome in December 1911. The rebels proclaimed a new Republic of China with Sun Yat-sen chosen as provisional president. More than 2,000 years of monarchy in China had come to an end.

For the builders of the new Chinese republic, however, it proved to be a false start. Sun found himself in the position of a leader with lots of prestige but

With their private armies, "warlords" used most of their energy in a cruel competition for power and wealth.

almost no power. He had no working political organization within China. And he didn't have an army that was loyal to him personally.

Against Sun was an aging and ambitious general by the name of Yuan Shih-kai,* commander of the Manchu imperial army and the last Manchu prime minister. Since Yuan's power was far greater than Sun's, the two leaders made a deal. Yuan accepted the new republic, and Sun stepped down as president. Yuan took his place.

Yuan's ambition was to restore the monarchy, with himself as the founder of a new ruling dynasty. But when his own generals balked at the idea, Yuan had to backtrack. A disappointed Yuan died in 1916.

Yuan's death, however, left China without any effective central government at all. Power passed to the governors and military chiefs of the individual provinces. Thus began the era of the "warlords." With their private armies, they used most of their energy in a cruel competition for power and wealth. Their ragtag soldiers often behaved like bandits, more interested in pillaging peasant villages than in providing for public safety.

With China rapidly disintegrating, Sun Yat-sen once more tried to put the pieces back together. Now his instrument of national reunification would be a new political party called the *Kuomintang,** the "National People's Party," or Nationalist Party.

Sun proclaimed his Nationalist government the legal government of all China. He asked the U.S. and the major powers of Europe for official recognition and aid in money. But he never got a clear-cut answer. The Western countries often seemed to be

The year: 1927. A warlord army tramps unfeelingly through a peasant's field near Canton.

147

more interested in preserving their investments and privileges in China than in supporting a man who might bring sweeping changes.

There was, however, one foreign government which was willing to assist Sun: the new Communist government of the Soviet Union. In 1917 the Communists of Vladimir Lenin emerged triumphant from the Russian Revolution and then survived a bitter civil war to establish the world's first Communist state. Flushed with success, Soviet leaders began to lay the groundwork for spreading communism to neighboring China.

Sun Yat-sen was not himself a Communist. But he accepted Soviet supplies and advisers to organize, train, and equip a new Nationalist army. He also agreed to accept members of China's own Communist Party into his movement. The two parties were not merged. But Chinese Communists were allowed to join the Kuomintang as individuals.

Sun did not live to realize most of his hopes for a new China. In 1925, while in Peking to persuade the northern warlords to accept his government, Sun died. He never ruled China. And a half century after his death his dream of a strong, fully united China was not yet achieved. But his life's work in the cause of the Republic of China has never been forgotten by those who followed him. To them he remains the "father of the Chinese Republic," China's first national hero in modern times.

Double-check

Review

1. Give two reasons for the spread of Western ideas in China in the early 20th century.

2. Where was Sun Yat-sen when a major revolt broke out in China? When did he return to his country?

3. What was the *Kuomintang*?

4. What was the reaction of Western countries when Sun Yat-sen asked them for recognition and aid?

5. How long did Sun Yat-sen rule a united China?

Discussion

1. Using what you have learned in previous chapters, try to answer the questions that confronted China's leaders and thinkers at the start of the 20th century: Why couldn't China resist the challenge of Western imperialism? What made the foreign powers so strong? How could China come to terms with the forces of the modern world?

2. Using Sun Yat-sen as your primary example, explain your answer to this question: Do leaders create history or does history create leaders?

3. What might have happened in China if the Communists had not sent supplies and advisers to train and equip the Nationalist army?

Activities

1. One student might play the role of Sun Yat-sen asking the U.S. and major powers of Europe for official recognition and financial aid for his new Nationalist government. Three other students could play the roles of skeptical diplomats representing the U.S. and two other nations.

2. Some students might draw editorial cartoons of the meeting between Sun Yat-sen and Yuan Shih-kai, with Sun representing China's future and Yuan representing China's past.

3. Some students might pretend they are Sun Yat-sen in 1925. Write his last entry in his diary about his own life and what he thinks will happen to China when he dies.

Skills

STEPS TOWARD A MODERN CHINA

1866	A. A major revolt explodes in China.
1879	B. Sun Yat-sen is born near Canton.
1883	C. Yuan Shih-kai takes over as president.
1884	
1894	D. Sun goes to Hawaii to be educated.
1896	E. Sun organizes a secret revolutionary society.
1911	F. Rebels proclaim a new Republic of China.
1911	
1912	G. Sun returns home at age 17.
1916	H. Sun goes to Hong Kong to become a doctor.
1923	I. Yuan dies; warlords take over China.
1924	J. Sun is kidnapped by the Chinese in London.
1925	K. Nationalists become the legal government of China.
	L. Sun dies while in Peking.
	M. Communists supply the Nationalist army.

Chapter 14 describes each of the events listed above. The exact years in which some of the events took place are given in the chapter. For other events, you can figure out the years from other information in the chapter. For still other events, the only clue to their dates is the order in which they happened. By using the timeline above and going back through the chapter, try to do the following things on a separate sheet of paper.

1. Write the years given above down the left-hand side of your paper.

2. Using the dates and the clues in the chapter, write the letter of each event above next to the year in which it happened. (The events are *not* in the correct order in the list above.)

Chapter 15

The General

SUN'S SUCCESSOR to the Kuomintang leadership was a young army officer named Chiang Kai-shek. His name would be the most prominent one on the China scene for the next 25 years.

Chiang was born to a merchant family which, by Chinese standards, was fairly well off. Though his early training was in the traditional Chinese classical pattern, he decided in his teens to become a soldier.

While in his 20's, Chiang joined Sun's Kuomintang movement in Canton. Chiang rose rapidly as a trusted military adviser to Sun. After a six-month visit to Moscow to study the Soviet army, Chiang was named superintendent of a new military college set up near Canton with Soviet help to train officers for Sun's Nationalist army.

After Sun's death the mantle of Kuomintang leadership fell to Chiang as the party's military chief. His first act was to begin the military unification of the

The year: 1939. Generalissimo Chiang Kai-shek
emphasizes a point during a speech to his army.

country. From Canton the Nationalist army marched through one province after another, seizing control from the warlords. Agents, both Kuomintang and Communist, paved the way for Chiang's army by promoting peasant revolts and desertions among the armies of the warlords.

Yet, even as the Nationalist-Communist alliance drove on to victory over the warlords, a fierce power struggle raged within its own ranks. There were three opposing groups. First there were the Communists.

Then the non-Communist majority within the Kuomintang was itself split into two factions: a "left wing" which urged continued alliance with the Communists, and a "right wing" which wanted the Communists expelled.

The Kuomintang's right wing struck first. Thousands of Communists or "suspects" in Shanghai were arrested and quickly executed. The Soviet advisers in the Kuomintang were expelled and sent home.

Chiang Kai-shek emerged as the most powerful man in China. With most of China in the hands of Chiang's Nationalists, the foreign powers finally recognized Chiang's regime as the national government of China.

Pockets of Communist resistance remained, however. Communist attempts to seize control of cities in the south were easily crushed by Nationalist forces. But the Communists were more successful in the countryside. In the rugged mountains of Kiangsi* Province, a young Communist organizer by the name of Mao Tse-tung had begun to establish a stronghold.

In 1930 Chiang's Nationalist armies began a series of campaigns designed to mop up the Communist forces. But the campaigns failed. And the rebel forces grew in numbers.

In late 1933 the Nationalists devised a new strategy. They set up a "starve-them-out" blockade of the Communist area, encircling the rebels with a ring of forts and strongpoints. After a year of the blockade, Chiang's Nationalists were on the verge of total victory — when the Communists suddenly broke out of the trap.

They began a zigzagging 6,000-mile retreat to escape the pursuing Nationalists. Despite staggering losses, a battle-hardened corps of Communists survived the year-long ordeal — the famous "Long

The year: 1937. Triumphant Japanese troops march through a captured Chinese village. Many people say that World War II began with the Japanese attack on Pearl Harbor on December 7, 1941. What do you think of this statement?

✑ Within China a great outcry arose
for a united effort to meet the
Japanese threat. "Chinese must not
fight Chinese," said a popular slogan.

March" — to find haven in north-central China. There, patiently and steadily, Mao Tse-tung rebuilt his forces.

Perhaps if Chiang's Nationalists had had more time, they might have destroyed the Communists. And perhaps then Chiang could have gone on from there to bring about a basic change in China.

But Chiang wasn't given the time. Even as he sought to crush the Communist threat within China, his nation was confronted with a growing outside threat: Japan.

The Japanese had been a threat in Manchuria for many years, seeking to harness the area's natural resources for Japan's growing economy. But in 1931 the Japanese decided to conquer Manchuria by force. Japanese forces struck suddenly in September 1931. Within a few months they had gained complete control over Manchuria. Within China a great public outcry arose for a new united Chinese effort to meet the Japanese threat. "Chinese must not fight Chinese," said a popular slogan. The Communists too proposed a renewed alliance — a joint "patriotic war" against the Japanese.

The Japanese government took one look at the trend toward a new Nationalist-Communist alliance in China — and promptly launched a full-scale invasion. In a matter of days, the Japanese had overrun much of northern China. By the end of 1937, the Japanese had taken control of much of China's coast.

Now it was Chiang who was faced with making a

heroic retreat. Though most of coastal China was in Japanese hands, Chiang stubbornly refused to surrender. The Nationalist government moved westward ahead of the Japanese army, finally establishing itself in Chungking deep in China's interior. Libraries, art treasures, machinery, and even whole factories were packed up and dragged inland on boats or on the backs of men. Chiang's regular armies fought to delay the Japanese offensive, often burning and flooding fields. Chinese guerrilla armies struck at enemy supply and communications lines.

By 1940 the war had reached a stalemate. The Japanese had all the big coastal cities, the lower Yangtze Valley, Manchuria, and most of northern China. They were in control of 95 percent of China's modern industry and transportation facilities. Figuring that was just about all they could do in China, the Japanese turned in other directions.

On December 7, 1941, the Imperial Japanese Navy launched a devastating surprise attack on the U.S. Naval Base at Pearl Harbor in Hawaii: The U.S. had been plunged into World War II.

Suddenly China found itself with a whole bunch of new allies in the struggle against Japan. Convinced that the Allies would inevitably defeat the Japanese, Nationalists and Communists in China turned their primary attention from fighting the Japanese to the future fight against each other. Both sides sought to save their strength and resources. For both knew that their civil war was only temporarily called off.

Sure enough, after Japan surrendered to the Allies in 1945, the desperate struggle between Nationalists and Communists for control of China resumed. At first Chiang's Nationalists appeared to have the upper hand. Chiang had worldwide popularity as a symbol of Chinese resistance to Japan during World War II.

JAPAN OCCUPIES CHINA (1930-1945)

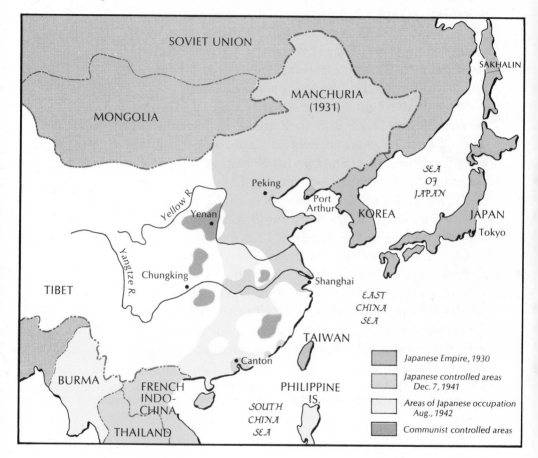

Map legend:
- Japanese Empire, 1930
- Japanese controlled areas Dec. 7, 1941
- Areas of Japanese occupation Aug., 1942
- Communist controlled areas

His government had been given a permanent seat on the new United Nations Security Council. His army, including more than a dozen crack divisions trained and equipped by the U.S., was four to five times bigger than that of the Communists.

But the Nationalist government was in deep trouble. It sought to regain control over a land exhausted and devastated by years of warfare. The

157

strain of maintaining such a large army brought on a raging inflation which reduced money to almost worthless scraps of paper. (In one two-year span, prices doubled and redoubled 67 times.) The long years during World War II when the Nationalists had been deep in China's interior regions had left them out of touch with the common people of China.

Most of the fighting in the early stages of the renewed Chinese civil war took place in Manchuria. There, with large quantities of captured Japanese weapons given to them by the Soviet army, Mao's Communists gradually bottled up Chiang's armies. Besieged and cut off, entire Nationalist divisions deserted en masse to the Communists. By 1948 all of Manchuria was in the hands of Mao's forces.

Chiang's Nationalists, weakened by corruption and disorganization, collapsed with astonishing speed in the face of a disciplined Communist onslaught. At the end of 1949, Chiang and what was left of his government and armies fled the Chinese mainland. On the offshore island of Taiwan,* the Nationalists set up a rival regime to the People's Republic of China (see Chapter 19). Chiang was still president of that regime when he died in 1975 at the age of 87.

Double-check

Review

1. What was Chiang Kai-shek's first act after assuming leadership of the Kuomintang?

2. What role did advance agents play in the battles between the Nationalist-Communist alliance and the Chinese warlords?

3. What event renewed the possibility of a Nationalist-Communist alliance in 1931?

4. What happened to the United States on December 7, 1941?

5. When did the Nationalist forces flee the Chinese mainland, and where did they go?

Discussion

1. Chiang Kai-shek studied in Moscow, headed a college set up with Soviet aid, and fought together with Communists to defeat Chinese warlords. Then thousands of Communists or "suspects" were arrested and executed, and Soviet advisers in the Kuomintang were expelled. Chiang emerged as the most powerful man in China. What in China's history might have contributed to this course of events? Was Chiang a Chinese hero or an ungrateful opportunist? Explain.

2. What reasons might explain why the U.S. and other Western powers did not go to war with Japan when it invaded China?

3. Japan occupied large areas of China for several years in the 1930's and 1940's. In the 1970's, the two nations began to negotiate trade and other agreements. Do you think the Chinese people will ever trust Japan fully? How would you feel toward a country that invaded the U.S.? How long would those feelings last? Give reasons for your answers.

Activities

1. Several students might role-play a meeting in the early 1930's at which Communist and Nationalist Chinese discuss a renewed alliance to fight a "patriotic war" against the Japanese invaders.

2. Some students might research and report to the class on U.S. relations with China during World War II.

3. Some students might pretend they are Chiang Kai-shek in 1975. Write his last diary entry about his own life and China's future.

Skills

INVASION AND OCCUPATION

Use the map, "Japan Occupies China (1930-1945)," in Chapter 15 to answer the following questions.

1. What color are the parts of China that were not controlled by Japan at any time during this period?

(a) gray   (b) dark orange   (c) white and brown

2. Which of these areas was *not* part of the Japanese Empire in 1930 but *was* controlled by Japan by 1931?

(a) Taiwan   (b) Burma   (c) Manchuria

3. How many Communist-controlled areas were completely surrounded by the Japanese in 1942?

(a) one   (b) two   (c) three

Use the map in Chapter 15 and the map in Chapter 13 to answer the following questions.

4. What part of China that was taken over by Russia in 1898 was under Japanese control by 1930?

5. What part of China went to a European country in 1884 and was called by a different name by 1930?

Chapter 16

The Chairman

ON OCTOBER 1, 1949, Mao Tse-tung stepped up to a battery of microphones on the balcony of the main gateway to Peking's old Imperial City. A cheering crowd fell silent. Mao, his voice wavering a bit from the emotions of the moment, proclaimed a new People's Republic of China.

For China's new strong man, the road to victory was a lifetime of almost nonstop struggle and rebellion. Mao was born in 1893 to a peasant family that was considered fairly prosperous compared to neighboring families. As a youth, he had been an avid reader, something which brought him into frequent conflict with his father, who considered most activities not directly related to earning a living a waste of time. But young Mao argued that an education would enhance his future earning power, so his father allowed him to pursue an education. Mao had an uneven school record, excelling in social studies and the

*A youthful Mao Tse-tung is shown, left, talking
to peasants in the mountain districts of Yenan.*

study of Chinese classics, but doing poorly in science.
He also became a physical-fitness buff, and his fondness for swimming and taking long hikes would later
serve him well.

In 1918, when he was 25, Mao got a job as an assistant librarian at the Peking National University.
Surrounded by all that reading material, he again de-
voured books and newspapers. Mao later said that his
job in the library was "so low" that hardly anyone
even noticed he was there. Still he attracted the attention of the head librarian, who just happened to be
a founder of the Chinese Communist Party.

With his skill as an organizer, Mao soon rose to a position of power in the Chinese Communist Party. But Mao had a basic disagreement with some of his Communist colleagues. Most of them believed that the spearhead of any Communist movement had to be the workers who toil in factories. Mao, however, believed that China's millions of peasants should be the main focus of the Chinese Communist movement. He knew that China's long oppressed peasantry was once more ripe for revolt. Mao wrote a report on his idea, but he was sharply criticized by the party leadership.

When the Nationalists turned on the Communists in 1927, Mao had a chance to test his idea. He led his peasant force into mountainous Kiangsi Province. Mao expanded his control and was joined by other Red units that had escaped the Nationalist purge. He built up his forces with recruits from local villages.

Mao's guerrilla army fought Chiang Kai-shek's forces to a standstill until 1934. In that year Chiang launched an enormous offensive to destroy the Communists. For Mao the choice came to staying at his base in Kiangsi and being wiped out — or making a break for it. He decided to make the break.

So began the "Long March." Mao's columns zigzagged some 6,000 miles on foot into the deep interior of north-central China. They scaled 18 major mountain ranges, crossed dozens of deep rivers, slogged through many forests and swamps — all while fighting off the Nationalists. In the end, less than one fourth of those who started the Long March survived to reach their hideaway at Yenan* in Shensi* Province.

Mao's leadership through the difficult Long March confirmed his role as China's top Communist. Now his forces braced themselves for the next blow by

handwritten: 24 rivers 18 mountains

⊷ Mao's columns scaled 18 major ranges, crossed dozens of rivers, slogged through forests and swamps — all while fighting off the Nationalists.

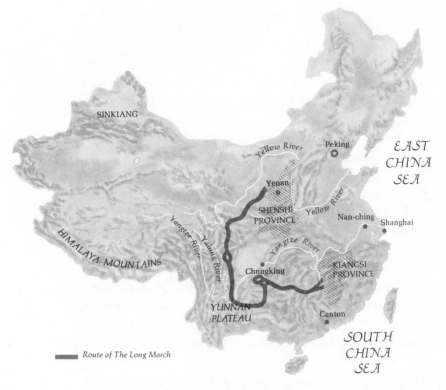

Route of The Long March, 1934-1935 ·

SINKIANG

Yellow River Peking

EAST
CHINA
SEA

Yenan

SHENSHI
PROVINCE Yellow River

Nan-ching Shanghai

Yangtze River

HIMALAYA MOUNTAINS Yangtze River Yalung River Yangtze River

Chungking KIANGSI
PROVINCE

YUNNAN
PLATEAU Canton

SOUTH
CHINA
SEA

▬ *Route of The Long March*

*The Long March was one of the great escapes of
history. Harried at every step by Chiang's
army, Mao's Communists zigzagged some 6,000
miles to Yenan, deep into the interior of China.
Left, Mao's weary men are shown slogging
across the snowy mountains of central China.*

Chiang's forces. But it never came. The war with
Japan once again made Chinese Nationalists and
Chinese Communists uneasy allies.

The Communist support Mao had helped to build
among China's peasants proved his major strength in
the renewed Chinese civil war after the end of World
War II. Mao's forces first defeated Chiang's National-

165

ists in Manchuria and then moved south, city by city, river by river, until they had conquered all of mainland China.

Thus, in 1949, the Chinese Communists took control of mainland China. As was so often the case in China's past, a major changeover in ruling regimes was accompanied by ruthless suppression. Perhaps no one will ever know precisely how many Chinese lost their lives as the Communists built up their power. Estimates range from several hundred thousand to many millions killed.

But the Chinese Communists also placed stress on persuasion — through thought control, propaganda, and group pressures — to force individuals to conform. The object was to develop a new sort of person in China, obedient to the state and dedicated to serving the new Chinese society.

The first years of Mao's rule brought a degree of national unity and internal peace that China had not known for at least a century. China began making real gains toward becoming a modern industrial state. The Communists launched programs for new factories, mines, steel mills, railroads, highways, power stations, and dams. New schools, hospitals, clinics, and housing projects sprang up in encouraging numbers.

Yet, as China's new leaders knew, the modernization of the country depended on modernizing the countryside. So Mao's Communists started a social revolution in the countryside to break up China's traditional patterns of life. It was called the "Great Leap Forward."

Drastic measures were ordered. Factories and mines were given high production schedules. This meant that workers had to work harder and put in longer hours. Farming communes (see Chapter 18) were formed in the countryside. Families were often

When the Communists took over the city of Nan-ching in 1949, curious citizens came out to get a look at the new conquerors. What emotions do you see in the faces of the people?

broken up (husbands and wives living in separate dormitories and children living in nurseries). Farmers ate in commune dining halls and marched to work in military formations. Their work day was from dawn to dusk, with breaks only for military drills and propaganda lectures.

But the "Great Leap" did not work. The commune system, for example, attacked one of the deepest of Chinese traditions — respect for the family. Because of this, it was opposed by many Chinese peasants. So, a year after launching the "Great Leap Forward," the Chinese Communists stepped back, easing many of the pressures on the Chinese people.

In the aftermath, Mao's prestige seemed to slip. Though he remained Chairman of the Communist Party, he gave up his post as head of the government.

Still he was not ready to take a back seat. A poet as well as a political leader, Mao wrote a poem in 1965 with these lines:

Nothing is difficult in this world
If you can keep climbing.

And in the mid-1960's his prestige began to climb, once again, with the "Great Proletarian Cultural Revolution." A massive propaganda campaign proclaimed Mao as world communism's leading light. Champion Ping-Pong players attributed their success in international tournaments to the inspiration of Chairman Mao's thoughts. China's air force pilots claimed they didn't need radar since they were guided by the thoughts of Chairman Mao.

Millions of Chinese youths, freed from the classrooms, were organized into Red Guard units and told to "learn revolution by making revolution."

Red Guard posters proclaimed that all traces of China's Confucian traditions, of foreign influence, of capitalism were to be stamped out. Red Guard mobs destroyed temples and churches, ransacked stores and homes. They beat or humiliated government officials who were not "revolutionary" enough.

But Mao's "turned-on" young revolutionaries were very hard to turn off. Red Guard harassment disrupted factory and farm production. Competing Red Guard groups began bloody battling with each other.

At this point, the People's Liberation Army had to

be called in. Schools reopened, and students were told to end the turmoil. The Great Proletarian Cultural Revolution was over.

A period of apparent calm descended on China. The government sought to improve its relations with the non-Communist world, including the U.S.

Wearied by years of struggle and fighting, Mao returned to semiretirement. He appeared in public only rarely. But he continued to dominate events in China.

During the turmoil of the Cultural Revolution, Mao had written: "The present Great Cultural Revolution is only the first. All members of the Communist Party and the people of the whole country must not think that everything will be all right after one or two great Cultural Revolutions, or even after three or four."

And by 1974, there were signs that another Cultural Revolution had indeed begun. This time, however, the struggle took place mainly behind locked doors, among government leaders.

The most revolutionary group was led by Chiang Ching,* Mao's wife. The "villains," in her eyes, were those officials who wanted China to settle down and make economic gains. Their leader was a deputy premier named Teng Hsiao-ping.*

Mao may not have supported his wife's extreme views, but he didn't want to see China settle down. Teng was thrown out of the government.

The revolutionaries had won—for the moment. But the stage was set for a bitter clash after Mao left the scene.

In September 1976, Mao died, at the age of 83. For more than 50 years he had carried on a revolution to promote communism in China. For better or worse, the son of the peasant had left his mark on China. His mark may prove as deep as those of any of China's mighty celestial emperors.

Double-check

Review

1. What was Mao's basic disagreement with most of his Communist colleagues?

2. How long was the Long March? How many of those who started it survived to reach Yenan?

3. What was the "Great Leap Forward"? What was a principal cause of its failure?

4. Who were the Red Guards? What were they told to do?

5. Who was the leader of the most revolutionary group of government officials in 1974?

Discussion

1. How were Mao Tse-tung's background and personality similar to and different from those of Sun Yat-sen and Chiang Kai-shek? Could these men have exchanged places successfully? Why, or why not? Which leader do you think did the most good for China? Why?

2. As leader of China, Mao encouraged his "deification," almost as if he believed he was a god. Did this seem silly, useful, or necessary in light of Chinese traditions? Explain your answer.

3. What does the rise and fall of the Red Guards suggest about maintaining and controlling the "spirit of revolution"? Was there a basic flaw in the idea of learning revolution by making revolution? Why, or why not?

Activities

1. Three students might role-play a meeting in 1980 between Sun Yat-sen, Chiang Kai-shek, and Mao Tse-tung, during which they criticize each other's actions, tell what they would have done differently, and speculate on the future of China.

2. Some students might research and report to the rest of the class on the Long March, indicating on a large wall map the route and places where significant events occurred.

3. Some students might pretend that they are members of the Red Guard, writing letters home to their parents explaining what they are doing and why.

Skills

THOUGHTS FROM CHAIRMAN MAO

> *It often happens that the masses need a certain change, but they are not yet conscious of the need. In such cases, we should wait patiently. Otherwise we shall isolate ourselves. Unless the masses are willing, any kind of work that requires their participation will fail. There are two principles here:*
>
> *1. The actual needs of the masses, rather than what we imagine they need.*
>
> *2. The wishes of the masses, who must make up their own minds instead of our making up their minds for them.*
>
> — Mao Tse-tung (1893-1976)

Use the passage above and information in Chapter 16 to answer the following questions.

1. When Mao writes about "the masses," he means China's
   (a) landlords. (b) factory workers. (c) peasants.

2. When Mao uses "we," he means China's
   (a) Nationalists. (b) Communist Party members. (c) peasants.

3. According to the passage, what is the correct order for these steps?
   (a) Masses are aware that they need a change.
   (b) Masses need a change.
   (c) Masses work to bring about the change.
   (d) Masses want to take part in making the change.

4. Which of these statements best sums up the passage?
   (a) Might makes right.
   (b) The masses never know what they want or need.
   (c) A good leader knows how to follow.
   (d) Loyal followers never ask questions.

5
CHINA TODAY

Chapter 17

China Without Mao

ONE MAN led the Chinese Communists for half a century. For 27 of those years, he led the government of China. (The U.S. had six different Presidents in the same period.) Many Chinese came to look upon Mao as something of a god. They turned to his writings for inspiration. To see him in person, at a public ceremony in Peking, was the high point of many Chinese people's lives.

But, of course, Mao was not a god. He was a mortal man. And the People's Republic of China went through a crisis when he died.

The year of upheaval was 1976. It started with the death of Premier Chou En-lai,* who had long been Mao's right-hand man. Chou, a skilled diplomat, had smoothed away many conflicts between radicals and moderates. His influence would be missed in the months to come.

Deng Xiaping

Who would be the next premier? First in line seemed to be ~~Teng Hsiao-ping~~, who gave the eulogy at Chou's funeral. But Chiang Ching and other radicals were bitterly opposed to Teng. Suddenly Mao named his choice as premier: Hua Kuo-feng, head of China's police system.

From then on Mao was probably too ill to take any active part in government decisions. In September of 1976, he died, and the whole nation was swept up in a great display of mourning. Behind the scenes, however, the struggle between radicals and moderates was reaching a climax.

Before Mao's death, Hua had tried not to take sides. He had criticized Teng, but had not thrown in his lot with the radicals. He was certainly in no mood to let them push him aside.

The details of the struggle for power may never come to light. But one thing seems clear: It was the military that held the key to victory. Back in the 1960's, when the Red Guards went on their rampage, Mao had called on the army to bring them under control. Since then, the government leaders knew they needed the support of the army. And the army knew it too.

Having had to mop up one Cultural Revolution, the People's Liberation Army was not eager for another. It stood behind Hua. One month after Mao's death, Chiang Ching and three other leading radicals were arrested. The charge: plotting to seize power. Many radical officials throughout the country lost their posts.

Top right: This 1963 photo shows Mao in center, ~~Teng Hsiao-ping~~ to left of him, Chou En-lai third to right. Bottom right: Hua Kuo-feng, head of government after Mao, steps out on a visit to Rumania.

The top radicals, now branded the "Gang of Four," were blamed for all of China's problems since the Cultural Revolution. This sweeping accusation had a basis of truth. In the name of equality, bright students from the cities had been sent out to work on farms. Graduate schools had been closed down. In the factories, showing the right political outlook had been more important than working hard. In short, China's economy and education system had been headed for collapse. New measures were needed.

This was what Teng Hsiao-ping had been saying all along. And in 1977 Teng sprang back into the spotlight. Hua held the top post of Chairman, but now Deputy Premier Teng held the power.

How did Deng manage to bounce back again? The army, which had backed Hua against the radicals, thought even more highly of Teng. After all, Teng was an old-timer who had been on the Long March in the 1930's. Hua, 15 years younger, had missed all the Chinese Communists' early struggles.

Whatever was really happening behind the scenes, one result was clear. With Mao gone, China was turning in a new direction.

The two most crucial changes were those planned for the economy and the education system:

1. *The economy.* For years, farm and factory workers had been urged to follow the thoughts of Mao. This was supposed to make them not only good Communists but also productive workers. Yet production had lagged severely since the Cultural Revolution.

China's new leaders tried a different incentive: money. About two thirds of all industrial workers received a pay raise, the first sizable one in more than 20 years. In addition, bonuses were given to workers who performed especially well.

Farm workers were encouraged to keep or increase

China's hopes for boosting its economy depend heavily on oil production. Women work with men on a rig in the large Shengli oil field.

their own private plots of land, and they were allowed to sell crops. Many communes already had workshops for making their own tools and clothes. Now, if they wished, they could step up production and sell the surplus. With their extra earnings, communes might buy labor-saving machinery or a TV set, or build themselves a new school.

*English is an important subject in
China's schools today. This teacher in
Shantung province uses television to get her
message across to several classes at once.*

178

2. *Education.* China has never had enough high schools or colleges for more than a small minority of its young people. The best high schools and colleges have been in the big cities. Traditionally, China's city-dwellers have enjoyed better jobs and more comfortable lives than the peasants.

Mao had tried to change all that. He wanted the children of poor peasants to move to the head of the line for higher education. As for city children, they should go out into the countryside and learn to use their hands. It was wrong for a person to have a good education, said Mao, unless he or she was also a dedicated Communist.

This idea was pushed to extremes during the Cultural Revolution. Having a good education created suspicion. It was an almost certain sign of being a bad Communist. Many high schools and colleges were shut for months on end. Graduate schools stopped work altogether. For years, hardly anyone in China was being fully trained in science, technology, and other advanced skills.

The new leadership aimed to turn all these ideas around. It decided that China could prosper only with a high level of scientific and technical education. Once again, the key to higher education would be ability, not background. To get into a high school, and from there into a university, a Chinese boy or girl would have to pass stiff competitive exams.

In charting these new courses, China after Mao made another striking change. Mao had wanted China to be able to stand alone, without relying on foreign trade or aid. The new leaders saw economic growth as their first priority. To achieve it they opened their doors to goods and technical aid from non-Communist countries.

As Western businessmen and tourists flocked to

*Above, college students from China learn the
ins and outs of an American supermarket.
At left, American tourists watch potters at work
in China.*

China, many Chinese had their first glimpse of a different way of life. Some of them compared it with their own way of life and wondered why their leaders could not make further changes. On wall posters and at meetings in the big cities, there were calls for more "human rights" and "democracy" in China.

For a time, the government let people have their say, but then it clamped down on such demonstrations. Clearly, there were limits to the changes that the new leaders were prepared to make. They would drop some of Mao's most cherished aims, and they would welcome closer contacts with the non-Communist world. But they had no intention of altering the Communist form of government that had shaped the lives of China's millions for a third of a century.

Double-check

Review

1. In the struggle for power after Mao's death, what element of the government held the key to victory?

2. Who were the "Gang of Four"?

3. Which two elements of society seemed headed for the most crucial changes as China turned in a new direction?

4. What two things did Chinese citizens call for on wall posters and at meetings in big cities?

Discussion

1. Given China's educational traditions, did Mao's suspicions and changes make sense? Why, or why not? Do the educational changes of the new leadership sound like good ideas? Which do, and which do not? Why? What might Confucius say about them?

2. In what ways — if any — would China's recent history be different if Teng Hsiao-ping had not come into power? Give reasons for your answers.

3. As China opens its economy and educational system to new ideas, do you think it will become more like the West? If so, how? If not, why?

Activities

1. Some students might plan a one-month trip to China for your class. List the cities and other areas you would like to visit. Name the sites, works of art, buildings, etc., that you would like to see, the people you would want to talk to, and what you would ask them.

2. Some students might role-play a meeting in China between two members of your class and three Chinese students. One of the Chinese students might be a radical who is distrustful of outsiders; the others could be interested in learning about life in the U.S.

3. Some students might pretend to be Teng Hsiao-ping, writing his first diary entry after assuming leadership of China. Write briefly about what happened to him in the past and what he plans for China's future.

Skills

© 1978 Copley News Service

Use the political cartoon above and information in Chapter 17 to answer the following questions.

1. Whom does the man on the left represent?
(a) Sun Yat-sen   (b) Deng Hsiao-ping   (c) Mao Tse-tung

2. Where did this cartoon first appear?
(a) Chinese book   (b) U.S. newspaper   (c) wall poster

3. Why does the man on the left look surprised?
(a) He is dead.   (b) His "ideas" have been changed.
(c) Democracy is a woman.

4. What does the main point of this cartoon seem to be?
(a) Democracy is a woman.   (b) Chinese spelling is changing.
(c) Teng is changing China.

5. Which two sentences in Chapter 17 suggest that this cartoon might be a little misleading?

183

Chapter 18

Life in China Today

TSOU PING starts each day with a workout. Before breakfast, she jogs and performs some martial arts exercises. It is important that she keeps in shape both mentally and physically. At 14, she knows she has much to learn before she can reach her goal of becoming a doctor.

During the week, Tsou attends a boarding school. It is only a couple of miles from her family's farm near the ancient city of Sian, but it is a world apart. School is serious business. After a breakfast of bean milk, fried rolls, steamed bread, and porridge, Tsou is in class by 7:30. She studies math, physics, chemistry, and politics plus Chinese and English.

The school day lasts until 5 P.M., but students break for lunch and a nap. Afterwards, they may wind down with a game of ping-pong or badminton. Then there's dinner. Before lights-out at 9 p.m., Tsou studies a couple of hours. After the lights go out, the students share

For centuries muscle power has fueled the Chinese economy.

their plans and dreams. Tsou and her friends are concerned about passing examinations to get into a university. One of Tsou's roommates wants to be an engineer, the other a teacher. They know they are lucky to have the chance to go to school.

Week-ends, Tsou returns to the family farm. There she visits with her parents, three brothers, and two sisters. By modern Chinese standards, their family is very large. Today, Chinese families are encouraged to have only one child.

Tsou's family lives in a tile-roofed, adobe-style compound of buildings around a central courtyard. Chickens and pigs share the courtyard. The family has its own garden to supply food for its table.

The family is considered better off than most in the village because it has its own well. Over the past six years, the family income has doubled. The parents have used it to buy two television sets, two sewing machines, three electric fans, and a washing machine. Moreover, they can afford to let Tsou go to school during the week. She is their youngest child.

Tsou and her family can thank the policies of Deng Hsaio-ping for their new prosperity. By the 1980's, he reached out to the modern world. He called his policies a second revolution. Influences that had long been shut out were allowed in. With loans from the World Bank and International Monetary Fund, western technology was brought in. The Chinese got a real taste of free enterprise, although they didn't call it that. Technicians, rather than party officers, were allowed to make business decisions. Vocational and technical courses were added to the school curriculum. Some 40,000 college graduates were sent abroad to study, 15,000 to the United States.

Deng's goal was to bring China into the 21st century as a developing—rather than an underdeveloped—nation. The changes, he insisted, were necessary if China was to survive. Teng's critics said that his open door would let in many problems of the outside world. Teng did not disagree. But he believed China could fight these problems if it had to.

Few believed, however, that Teng would live into the 21st century. In 1986, he was 81 years old. Could he pass the second revolution to the next generation? It was hard to tell. Within the party, there were still many Maoists who criticized him. Would they start another Cultural Revolution? Teng's supporters were convinced that the success of modernization made that unlikely. After all, with each year there were fewer and fewer Chinese who could remember Mao or the Cultural Revolution.

China remained a dictatorship, and—Teng insisted— thoroughly communist. However, Western tourists who had visited China in the 1970's and returned in the 1980's were astonished at the changes everywhere. They found disco dancing, Japanese motorcycles, and Western television programs. The blue padded "Mao" jackets and trousers that were once a sort of revolution-ary uniform had given way to a colorful array of cloth-ing. Much of it was Western.

The changes began in the countryside. Eighty per-cent of the Chinese population lives in rural areas. In two generations, farmers had worked under drastically different systems. Before the Communist Revolution, Chinese farming was practically feudal. Peasants had rented small patches of land from a landlord. They paid him most of their crops as rent. Peasants never sent their children to school. When they were sick, there was no medicine. When they were hungry, they often starved.

The revolution ended the vast inequalities between landlords and peasants. Tiny farms were replaced by

*This is another picture for which you must
write your own caption. Look at it carefully,
for it holds a number of clues to understanding
the life-styles of a Chinese farm family today.*

huge *communes*. These were huge communities made
up of thousands of acres of land worked by hundreds of
families. Often families were split apart. Married cou-
ples lived in separate barracks, their children in a third.
They ate in public canteens and attended Communist
indoctrination meetings at night. The Cultural Revolution glorified farming, but education was suspect.

In a commune, everyone received a basic wage. But
those workers who put in extra hours in the fields or at
party meetings received "work points." The points were

supposed to make people better workers and better Communists. But they rewarded time spent rather than results. They did not lead to higher output.

Under Mao, everyone got to eat, but diets were often lacking in protein and adequate calories. China remained a poor country. In time, China's leaders saw that this system was not working. In 1976, China even had to import rice. If China was to feed its people well, some incentive was needed.

At first, the leadership let farmers build their own houses. Families were allowed to eat breakfast and dinner at home. Children were allowed to go to school, especially if they excelled. Best of all, families were given small plots to farm for themselves. On them they could raise crops to eat themselves or to sell.

By 1981, the commune system was mostly scrapped. The state still owned the land, but it leased it to small groups—mostly families. Farmers were allowed to decide what crops to grow. Once they paid their quota of crops—such as rice or wheat—to the government, they were free to market what remained. With the profits, they could buy more farm animals or even tractors. The animals and the equipment belonged to the farmers, not the state.

The new agricultural policies seemed to work. By 1985, China had produced a world's record grain harvest—407 million tons. Farmers were asked to produce less food. The state could no longer afford the bonuses it offered to spur production.

All over rural China, living standards improved. Mud-walled huts with straw roofs were replaced by brick cottages with tile roofs. Some villages even had apartment buildings. Like Tsou Ping's family, many farmers bought electrical appliances.

Tsou Ping's life is hard by U.S. standards. But it is a good one by China's standards. Her mother and father remember days when they went hungry as children.

How is city life different? The Chung family lives in Peking where Mr. Chung works in a truck plant as an

An assembly line for heavy trucks in Chang-ch'un.

assembly-line mechanic. Mrs. Chung cuts patterns at a clothing factory. Both work six days a week — never with a vacation. But the Chungs are considered well off, for both own bicycles, each one costing about three months' pay.

Every morning the Chungs ride their bikes to work. The truck plant and the knitting factory are about a mile from each other. The two Chungs pedal along tree-lined streets, past low buildings in the

A Peking street committee meets to plan work activities for everyone who lives on the block. At this meeting, the committee decided to manufacture cardboard boxes and sandals.

Outer City. Then they pass through the gates of the Inner City, where they put their bikes in parking lots and go in to their work.

Peking is laid out like boxes within boxes. Inside the Inner City is the Imperial City. Inside the Imperial City is the Forbidden City. This last, once forbidden to the common people, is now a series of parks, museums, and government buildings. High officials make their homes here.

At the entrance to Chung's plant is a poster saying, "Everyone must work as well as he can for his country." Below the poster is a bulletin board with pictures of outstanding workers. Having your picture on the bulletin board is considered a great honor.

On Wednesday afternoons, Chung must attend a meeting where politics and plant policies are discussed. The workers also take turns praising or criticizing one another for the way each one has done his job that week.

Chung's factory has a director as its head, but Chung must follow the orders of the Communist Party unit at the factory. The Party penalizes lazy workers and rewards good workers with both praise and medals.

After Mao's death, a new policy was introduced. Cash bonuses were given to workers who did overtime or put some extra effort into their jobs. For example, Mrs. Chung and her co-workers thought of a way to cut fabric for clothes with less waste. As a result, they all shared a 100-dollar bonus.

Mr. Chung belongs to a labor union, but it is a group without much power. In China the union does not take the side of the worker against management. Nor would it ever call a strike, as the government does not allow strikes.

As a skilled worker, Chung earns the equivalent of about 30 dollars a month. The plant director earns about twice as much, the beginner about half as much. When the Chungs combine their salaries, they have money enough to keep one daughter in primary school and another in middle school. They pay rent on a small apartment, buy food and a few changes of clothing, and own their bicycles.

Medical services are provided by the union. The Chungs will get small pensions when they retire. If they grow too old to take care of themselves, their children will certainly take good care of them — an age-old tradition in China.

The Chungs have never been outside Peking. Travelers need a special government pass, issued only for reasons such as a family emergency or a job transfer. They spend some of their leisure time in the Forbidden City and some of it at the opera, a favorite form of entertainment in China. In the old days, Chinese operas dealt with princes, emperors, and demons. Nowadays the opera stages are often filled with soldiers, peasants, workers, and Communist Party officials.

One opera, for example, tells the story of a fire-fighting company. The unit has both good and lazy firemen. The lazy ones cause a near-disaster, almost killing the bride of one of the firemen. At the last moment, she is rescued by a Communist Party secretary. The lazy firemen realize the error of their ways, and the Party secretary is hailed as the hero.

In recent years, the Chungs have had a somewhat wider choice of entertainment. Movies from the U.S. and other non-Communist countries may occasionally be shown. Western classical music — banned at the outbreak of the Cultural Revolution — has been heard again since Mao's death.

The Chungs also spend part of their leisure time at night school, learning English. They are proud of the fact that they could exchange at least some words with an American visitor.

Yet even if they spoke the same language, the Chungs and the American would be separated widely by experience and outlook.

Double-check

Review

1. How is Tsou Ping's daily life different from earlier generations of Chinese farm children? Why does she study so hard?
2. How is Tsou Ping's family better off than others in the village? How is it different from the model favored by the state?
3. What happened to the commune system under Teng's second revolution? How have Teng's policies affected factories?
4. How is the Forbidden City used now?

Discussion

1. Under Mao's leadership, nearly everyone in China dressed exactly alike, including men and women. Why do you think this was done? What are some advantages and disadvantages to such a custom, especially in light of ancient Chinese traditions?

2. Do you think the system of cash bonuses will cause Chinese workers to put extra effort into their jobs? How does this — or does this — fit in with other factors that motivate Chinese workers?

3. Why do you think Western classical music and other forms of outside culture were banned during the Cultural Revolution? Why do you think they are now being allowed back in? What effect — if any — might this have on Chinese people and culture?

Activities

1. A committee of students might collect stories and pictures about life in China today from newspapers and magazines, and post these on the bulletin board for discussion.

2. Several students might role-play a reunion between Mao and Teng. Teng might explain his reasons for China's modernization, and Mao might react.

3. The entire class might pretend that it has been asked by the U.S. government to select examples of U.S. culture to be sent to China next month. Other classes will be selecting works of art, books, drama, etc. Your class must select 10 records and five movies. Which ones would you send? Discuss the possibilities and then vote on the final choices.

Skills

WHEAT AND CORN PRODUCTION IN CHINA

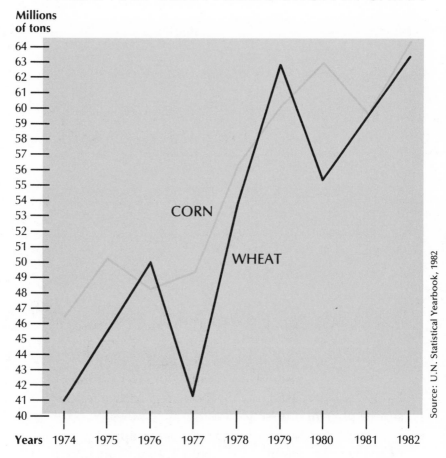

Source: U.N. Statistical Yearbook, 1982

Use the line graph above and information in Chapter 18 to answer the following questions.

1. What do the numbers on the left of the graph indicate? What are the numbers along the bottom of the graph?

2. Which crop has not increased steadily every year?

3. How many tons of corn were produced in 1979?

4. In what year was the production of wheat and corn nearly the same? In what year was there the greatest difference?

5. Would you say that the government's new agriculture policy is a success?

The Taiwan Tangle

PORTUGUESE SAILORS in the 16th century named it Ilha Formosa,* the "beautiful island." The Chinese call it Taiwan, meaning "terraced fields." Either way this leaf-shaped island set about 100 miles off mainland China's coast has long been regarded as a desirable piece of property.

A central mountain range with snowcapped peaks runs down the length of the island, leaving only about 25 percent of the area suitable for farming. But the climate is mild, the rainfall plentiful. Through intensive cultivation, Taiwan's farmers grow more than enough food to feed the island's fast-growing population. (Taiwan is one of the most densely populated places on earth.)

Taiwan had been a province of the Chinese empire for centuries until it was taken by Japan in the peace settlement ending the first Sino-Japanese War of 1894-95. With the defeat of Japan in World War II 50 years later, Taiwan was returned to Chinese con-

trol. For many Taiwanese it was not a happy return. When Chiang Kai-shek's Nationalists fled the mainland in 1949, Taiwan suddenly found itself host to more than 1.5 million mainland refugees fleeing the Communists.

On Taiwan, Chiang's Nationalists regrouped their shattered forces. Linked to the U.S. in a defense treaty, and supplied with more than 2.5 billion dollars in U.S. military aid, the Nationalists rebuilt their army into a modern, efficient fighting force. At the same time, the Chiang regime has worked to create a showcase society that would contrast with the drabness of life on the mainland. In a highly successful land reform program, for example, the government set a 7.5 acre limit on the land holdings of individuals. It bought up all excess lands and sold them to farmers at reasonable prices. By 1970 nine out of 10 Taiwanese farmers owned the land they worked.

Equally impressive gains have been made in many other areas: education, public health, industrial development, and foreign trade. In recent years Taiwan has enjoyed one of the highest economic growth rates in Asia. Much of this was due to the 1.5 billion dollars in U.S. economic aid sent to Taiwan during the 1950's and early 1960's. But in mid-1965, Taiwan's economy was judged strong enough to get along without further U.S. economic aid.

The boom and bustle of Taiwan is most evident in Taipei,* Taiwan's largest city and seat of the Chinese Nationalist government. With more than two million residents (seven times the population when the Nationalists arrived in 1949), Taipei is one of those

The bustle and excitement of urban living is clearly evident in Taipei. How would you compare this picture with the pictures in this book of urban life on the Chinese mainland?

places where a new building seems to go up every time you turn around. But urban growth also brings urban problems: traffic jams, pollution, and a kind of never-ending din.

Still, Taiwan's main problem is political. It remains the focal point of a dispute between two old Chinese enemies: the Communists and the Nationalists. To the Communists, Taiwan represents "unfinished business," a piece of China still to be "liberated." To the Nationalists, Taiwan is the base from which they hope to gain control of all China.

Added to this tangle is the friction between "native Taiwanese" (descendants of Chinese who immigrated to Taiwan over hundreds of years before 1895) and "mainlanders" (those who came after 1949). The "native Taiwanese" make up about four out of every five island residents. Many of them want a separate, independent Taiwan linked to *neither* the Communists *nor* the Nationalists. And while native Taiwanese have been given an expanded role in running local government, real political power remains firmly in the hands of mainland-born officials of the Nationalist regime.

What does the future hold for Taiwan? The Nationalists' dream of one day "retaking the mainland" grows dimmer every year. Chiang Kai-shek is dead (his son took over the presidency). China's seat in the United Nations has passed from the Nationalists to the Communists. The U.S. has cut its official ties with Taiwan and recognized the Communist government. Today only a handful of countries still accept the Nationalists' claim to represent all of China.

All the same, the Communists show no sign of planning to "liberate" Taiwan by force. Unofficial ties between the U.S. and Taiwan continue. In spite of the shadows that hang over it, Taiwan seems likely to survive and prosper for a long time to come.

Double-check

Review

1. What does *Taiwan* mean in English? *terraced fields*

2. How many Taiwanese farmers owned the land they farmed in 1970? *9 out of 10*

3. How much military and economic aid was given to Taiwan by the United States between 1949 and 1965? *1.5 billion $*

4. What kind of government would many "native Taiwanese" like to see developed in their country? *neither commy nor nationalist*

5. Who took over the presidency of Taiwan's Nationalist government when Chiang Kai-shek died? *his son*

Discussion

1. Do you think the Nationalist government on Taiwan should still be recognized as the one true government representing all of China? Why, or why not? Should it ever have been? Explain your answer.

2. Do you think U.S. government policy of cutting official ties to the Nationalists and recognizing the Communist government has lessened or increased the possibility of conflict between the two Chinese governments? What might trigger armed conflict? What might prevent it?

3. From what you have learned in previous chapters, would you imagine that traditional Chinese values and customs are stronger on Taiwan or on the mainland? Why?

Activities

1. Some students might pretend they are Chinese students in Taiwan writing a letter to relatives on the mainland explaining why they prefer to live in Taiwan. Other students might pretend to be students on the mainland writing to relatives in Taiwan explaining their preferences for life on the mainland. Afterward, some students might read their letters aloud.

2. One student might play the role of Nationalist China's delegate to the United Nations arguing that his or her government should retain its seat. Another student could play the role of a representative of the People's Republic arguing that his or her government should be given the seat.

3. Some students might form committees to research and report on various aspects of life on Taiwan. Possible topics might include: Remnants of Japanese Cultural Influences; Westernization of Taiwan; Democracy on Taiwan; Current U.S. Relations with Taiwan.

Skills

Use the map above and information in Chapter 19 to answer the following ~~DO~~ *questions.* ~~all~~

1. What body of water separates the main island of Taiwan from the People's Republic of China? *Formosa Strait*

2. About how many miles and in which direction would you travel to get from Fu-chou to the capital of Taiwan? *150   SE*

3. On which half of the main island do you think most Taiwanese farms are located? On what do you base your answer? *South   no Taipei*

4. Where do you think most of the mountains in Taiwan are located? On what do you base your answer?

SE   hat many town

201

Chapter 20

Chinese Outside China

THROUGHOUT THEIR LONG HISTORY, the Chinese people have tended to stay at home. Likewise China as a nation has tended to isolate itself from the rest of the world. China's pride has helped keep it out of circulation.

But many Chinese people have always had itchy feet. Their main reason for leaving China and migrating to other countries has been to increase their earnings. In China most of them could barely make ends meet. They hoped to find jobs or start businesses that would bring them better lives.

Today Chinese live in most major cities around the world. As newcomers many of them find it hard to enter the mainstream of city life. Unfamiliar with the language and the city's ways, they often live in local "Chinatowns." To earn money, many open hand laundries or small Chinese-style restaurants. Some work at home as tailors and seamstresses or at small assembly tasks. Often they do not mix easily with their non-Chinese neighbors.

In the U.S., however, most of the children of Chinese immigrants attend public schools and become part of the community. Many go to college and follow successful careers. Some have become notable scientists, artists, or businessmen.

The first flood of Chinese into the United States took place just after gold was discovered in California in 1848. Word soon reached China (as it did the rest of the world) that riches were to be had for the taking in the California hills. By 1851 there were about 25,000 Chinese in search of their fortunes in the *Gum San** — the "Golden Mountains." A few struck it rich, but most found nothing but trouble. They fell easy victims to other miners, who often robbed and roughhoused them in the wild and lawless mining camps.

The next great surge of Chinese into the United States came only a few years later. The Central Pacific Railroad, ready to lay track for the Western segment of the first transcontinental railroad, put out a call for laborers. Shiploads of young Chinese peasants came over in response to the call. They tunneled through mountains or leveled them, blasting rock and earth, working hard to prove their worth. The job was done when the Central Pacific linked up with the Union Pacific at Promontory, Utah, in 1869.

Most of the now-jobless Chinese drifted back to the West Coast, especially San Francisco. They huddled in little Chinatowns and got the undeserved reputation of being opium-smoking criminals. Nearly all were poor and uneducated.

When California was swept by a series of financial panics in the 1870's, the Chinese became the scapegoats. The new labor unions charged that the use of "cheap coolie labor" was dragging down the living standards of "honest American workers."

Immigrant Chinese laborers provided much of the muscle power for first U.S. transcontinental railroad. The 1877 photo shows road being pushed through California's Sierra Nevada mountains.

"The Chinese Must Go" became the rallying cry of the Workingmen's party in California. The party didn't succeed in sending the Chinese home, but it did pressure Congress into passing the Chinese Exclusion Act of 1882. The act barred most Chinese immigration to the United States for 10 years. Renewals of the act kept the Chinese out for the next half century.

A turnabout came in World War II. As a wartime ally, China won the respect of the United States, and Americans began to regard Chinese in a new light. The Chinese Exclusion Act was repealed, and a token quota of 105 Chinese immigrants a year was set up. After the Communists took over mainland China in

1949, the United States admitted Chinese refugees far beyond the quota. And in 1965 the United States eliminated immigration quotas based on race or national origin.

Since then many Chinese from Taiwan, Hong Kong, and Southeast Asia — plus a trickle from the People's Republic — have settled in the United States. Like members of other ethnic groups, they enjoy recalling their old culture and history and blending those ways with the ways of their new land.

But the more than 16 million Chinese who live in the turbulent countries of Southeast Asia don't have quite the same attitude toward their governments as the Chinese-Americans do. Historians and journalists call these people "overseas Chinese." They call themselves *hua-chiao,** meaning "sojourning Chinese."

A sojourner is a kind of visitor. He or she is there for a while, but doesn't mean to stay forever. That's the way the majority of overseas Chinese, even those who have been in Southeast Asia for generations, regard themselves.

It's true that many have married natives of the lands they live and work in. Some have forgotten their Chinese language, or as children had never learned it. Nevertheless, most Chinese in Southeast Asia never get over the idea that their stay is temporary. Some day, they feel, they'll either want to leave — or be forced to.

The Chinese began to go to Southeast Asia many hundreds of years ago. By the 1500's there were Chinese traders in many Southeast Asian communities. The area really didn't open up to the Chinese, however, until European nations established colonies in the 1800's.

Most poor Chinese started their careers in Southeast Asia as laborers for the Europeans. But

Wherever they have gone, the Chinese have taken their distinctive foods with them. Above, a fish market in a Chinese section of Singapore.

many saved their money and soon set themselves up as businessmen. In many colonies the Chinese became merchants, operating the trade between the colony and the European colonial powers. Today these Chinese, or their children or grandchildren, own many of the shops and stores, hotels, and wholesale houses in the cities of Southeast Asia. They control rice markets also. They own rubber plantations, tin mines, and teak forests. Some overseas Chinese, wheeling and dealing on the international markets, are immensely rich. And some, for that very reason, are deeply resented by the peoples of the countries in which they live.

Mr. Fong would never allow either of his daughters to marry anyone but a Chinese. Nor would the girls disobey their father.

Many, however, remain poor. They toil as stevedores on the docks in Singapore or pedal pedicabs in Rangoon.

Rich or poor, the overseas Chinese tend to keep out of the politics of the country they are "sojourning" in. Except in Singapore, which has a Chinese prime minister and a population nearly 80 percent Chinese, the hua-chiao try to avoid calling attention to themselves. Most of them don't want to "make waves," that is, stir up controversy.

Instead of offering their first loyalty to the country they live in, most overseas Chinese are primarily loyal to China. But the question is — which China?

Some favor the Nationalist government on Taiwan. But now that the People's Republic represents China in the United Nations, many overseas Chinese give it their sole allegiance. Those loyal to the People's Republic aren't necessarily Communists. (There are, however, a number of dedicated Chinese Communists in every Southeast Asian country. They plot to install Communist governments — by legal means or by force.) Rather, they feel that the People's Republic is their ancestral home, the land where they have their roots.

That's the attitude of the Fong family, which lives in Kuala Lumpur,* the capital of Malaysia. Mr. Fong was born in Kuala Lumpur, the son of a Chinese

In the Chinese section of Kuala Lumpur, a Chinese wedding brings a crowd of onlookers.

laborer in the nearby teak forests. When it came time to marry, Mr. Fong never considered taking a Malay wife. The Malays are Moslems, and the Fongs — like most Chinese — follow a blend of Buddhism and Taoism, with a dash of the philosophy of Confucius.

Instead Mr. Fong returned to China for his bride. After an elaborate wedding ceremony, he brought her back to Kuala Lumpur to live. The Fongs have two teen-age daughters, Mei-ling and Su-chan.

Mr. Fong keeps a general store, selling all kinds of wares. On the counters in front of his shop, he offers a tempting array of foods — squid and dried fish, eggs and dried birds' nests, rice, preserved fruits from the People's Republic, spices of all kinds, pickles, crackers, cookies, canned beer, and a host of other items. Tucked away on his shelves and crammed below his counters are dishes and bottles and containers of all sorts, brooms and brushes, plastic sandals and umbrellas — an unimaginable variety of goods.

Over the shop, on a second story, are three sunny rooms where the Fongs live. Unlike the chock-full store, the apartment is sparsely furnished. Mr. and Mrs. Fong sleep in one room, the girls in a second, with the third serving as kitchen and living room.

Nearly a third of the people of Malaysia are Chinese, so the Fongs have plenty of friends. Mr. Fong would never allow either of his daughters to marry anyone but a Chinese. Nor would the girls do anything to disobey their father. Although they have never seen China, they live by Chinese custom and tradition.

The Fongs, of course, obey all Malaysian laws. But they also obey a "higher law" — one established by centuries of devotion to Chinese ancestors and China itself. The Malaysian laws are subject to change. To the Fongs, the Chinese "higher law" is eternal.

The peak above Hong Kong Harbor gives a bird's eye view of the many contrasts between old and new in the colony.

HONG KONG, COLONY IN FLUX

THE BRITISH ISLAND of Hong Kong perches on the edge of China. One of the world's leading financial centers, its government is very different from that of China. It encourages free enterprise. The theory is that if business is left on its own with little interference from the government, the economy will prosper. But China only leased Hong Kong to Great Britain, and that lease is up in 1997. In 1997, Hong Kong will officially come under Chinese rule.

Hong Kong is made up of the Kowloon Peninsula and the New Territories on the mainland of China, and more than 235 islands. Altogether it covers about 410 square miles. About 5.5 million people live in Hong Kong—12,537 people per square mile. This makes it one of the most densely populated areas in the world. Ninety-eight percent of Hong Kong's population is Chinese. Most are immigrants from southern China, or descendants of southern Chinese immigrants.

The colony of Hong Kong is built around one of the best

natural harbors in the world. In Chinese, the two words mean *fragrant harbor.* This harbor, along with the prospect of trade with China, first lured British merchants to Hong Kong in the 16th century. It wasn't until 1699 that the British managed to obtain a small trading settlement in Canton, 90 miles up the Pearl River from what is now Hong Kong.

Through this trading post China exported to Europe large quantities of tea, silks, furs, and porcelain. By comparison, it imported very little from Europe. To combat this trade imbalance, British and other European merchants began smuggling the addictive drug opium into China. Soon the tables were turned and the trade imbalance was in Great Britain's favor.

The influx of opium angered Chinese leaders and led to the Opium War in 1839. The war lasted for 14 months. As part of a peace agreement, the island of Hong Kong was ceded to Great Britain, but it was not until 1843 that the island was formally declared a British colony.

In 1984, after lengthy negotiations, Great Britain and China reached an agreement that will end British rule of Hong Kong and turn it over to China in 1997. Hong Kong will then become the Special Administrative Region of China.

The Chinese have agreed that the government will continue to be composed of local people, although the Chinese will appoint the chief executive. Freedom of the press, free assembly, and of religion are guaranteed. Hong Kong will remain a free port and financial center, and the Hong Kong dollar will still be legal money.

No one knows what the future will be like for the millions of Hong Kong residents when the colony is put under Chinese rule. Some people in Hong Kong are concerned that Chinese leaders may stray from the original agreement. China and Great Britain have different ideas about how to run a society. However, keeping Hong Kong's economy strong will be important to China. That makes many people confident that China and Hong Kong will be able to work together.

Double-check

Review

1. What was the main reason that many Chinese migrated to other countries?

2. When did the first flood of Chinese immigrants come to the United States? What brought the next great surge?

3. What was the Chinese Exclusion Act of 1882? How long did it affect Chinese immigration to the U.S.?

4. Who are the "overseas Chinese"? What do they call themselves?

5. How is the political involvement of the Chinese in Singapore an exception to the general behavior of Chinese people living in Southeast Asian countries?

Discussion

1. In what ways is the history of Chinese immigration to the U.S. similar to that of immigrants from European countries? In what ways is it different?

2. Why do you think Chinese immigrants in many countries "do not mix easily with their non-Chinese neighbors"? What aspects of Chinese culture might contribute to this? Why do many Chinese immigrants call themselves "sojourning Chinese" even after many years in a new country?

3. How do you think immigrants *to* China from other countries would be looked upon by the Chinese government?

Activities

1. A Chinese immigrant might be invited to speak to the class about his or her experience in the U.S. A committee of students might prepare a list of questions to give to the speaker in advance.

2. If there is a Chinese community in your city or nearby, some students might visit the markets, restaurants, art galleries, small shops, and other public places — and report pertinent observations to the class.

3. In 1979 many thousands of overseas Chinese were forced to flee Vietnam and other Southeast Asian countries. Some students might research and report to the class on those events and on the resettlement of the people who survived.

Skills

IMMIGRANTS TO THE U.S.

A. Numbers of Immigrants
Thousands

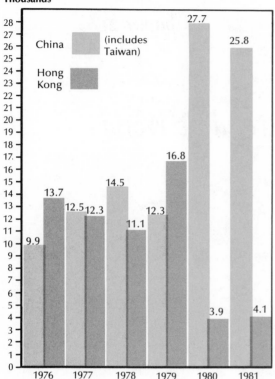

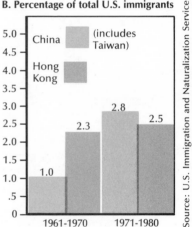

Source: U.S. Immigration and Naturalization Service

Use the bar graphs above and information in Chapter 20 to answer the following questions.

1. Where did the information in these graphs come from? Where are the figures for Taiwan?

2. What do the numbers on top of the bars in each graph mean?

3. In what years did the number of immigrants to the U.S. from China drop below the previous years?

4. From 1961-1970, a total of 3,321,700 came to the U.S. from all countries. Roughly how many of those (in numbers) were from China?

5. Using any of the years shown in Graph A, how many years would it take for the number of immigrants to the U.S. from China during these years to equal the number of Chinese immigrants who were in the United States in 1851?

Chapter 21

China and the World

IN THE 1950's, China had close ties with the Soviet Union and looked on the U.S. as its enemy.

In the 1960's, China still looked on the U.S. as its enemy but was now quarreling with the Soviet Union.

In the 1970's, China still quarreled with the Soviet Union but was now drawing closer to the U.S.

In the 1980's, China sought better relations with the Soviet Union as well.

What lies behind China's changing relations with the Soviet Union and the United States?

To answer these questions, we have to understand something about the nature of communism in China. And understanding "Chinese communism" requires a look at both words in this phrase. Communism originated in Europe, not in China. But like other foreign-originated ideas that made their way to China (Buddhism during a much earlier time, for instance), communism as practiced in China has taken on a distinctly Chinese flavor.

On the one hand, the leaders of the People's Republic of China are zealous Communists who talk of a global Communist revolution.

On the other hand, they are also fiercely Chinese. They share the painful memories of China's past. ("Our nation will no longer be an insulted nation," said Mao Tse-tung in 1949. "We have stood up.") They want to win for China a position of strength and leadership in the world.

One way to judge China's Communist leaders is by looking at the record to see how their actions stack up against their words. In each instance we might ask ourselves whether their actions reflect Communist revolutionary doctrine or Chinese nationalism. Or neither. Or both.

1. In 1950, when Communist North Korea invaded South Korea, a U.S.-led United Nations force rushed to the defense of South Korea. But as the U.S. counterattack rolled the North Koreans back toward the Manchurian border, China suddenly entered the fighting by sending some one million "volunteers" to save the North Korean regime. The result: a battlefield stalemate that led to a ceasefire in 1953.

2. In 1962 China and India fought a series of brief skirmishes along their poorly marked, long disputed boundaries in the Himalayan high country.

3. In 1969 and 1974, Russian and Chinese border units fired shots at one another. These clashes took place at remote spots on the northern rim of China.

4. In 1979 China invaded Vietnam, one of its southern neighbors. Vietnam, an ally of the Soviet Union,

A Chinese tank unit is awarded a banner for its part in the 1979 invasion of Vietnam.

had previously invaded Cambodia, an ally of China. According to the Chinese, the only purpose of their attack was to "punish" Vietnam.

Here are some other items that could be added to this list: (1) China's support of revolutionary "peoples' wars" in various parts of the world; (2) its four-million-strong People's Liberation Army which forms one of the world's largest fighting forces; and (3) Peking's refusal to sign an international treaty for banning nuclear tests in the atmosphere.

*Above, a peaceful display of China's strength
by athletes in Peking. The picture at rear
is made up of sections held by spectators.
At right, in the same stadium as above, Chinese
soldiers put on a not-so-peaceful display.*

All these items suggest an aggressive nation bent
on throwing its weight around. This is the way it can
appear from the outside looking in. Is the view different from the inside looking out?

China's leaders have complained of being encircled
by enemies. On the north is the might of the Soviet
Union. To the south are two Soviet allies, Vietnam and
Laos. To the southwest lies India, a nation second only
to China in population, with a government modeled
on Western democratic lines. Parked on the Pacific rim
of Asia is the power of the United States and its allies
(South Korea, Japan, and the Philippines). And then,
of course, there is Taiwan.

Some China analysts argue that the Chinese Communists haven't done anything which any strong Chinese government, Communist or otherwise, wouldn't

217

have done in similar circumstances. They view the Chinese intervention during the Korean War, the border disputes with India and the Soviet Union, even the invasion of Vietnam, as efforts by China to secure its national frontiers.

That China's Communist leaders hope to turn their nation into a modern power is hardly a secret. Which brings us to the next key question:

Could China's drive to become a world power involve it in angry confrontation — or even war — with one or the other of the world's two superpowers, the United States and the Soviet Union?

☆　☆　☆　☆　☆　☆　☆　☆　☆　☆

The Soviets greeted Mao's victory in China in 1949 with considerable satisfaction. Nevertheless, by the early 1960's, Moscow and Peking were openly feuding. One issue was revolutionary strategy. The Soviets believed that the Cold War (the struggle between the Communist bloc and the West) was getting too dangerous now that both sides were armed with nuclear missiles. The Communists of China disagreed. They wanted to keep up a tough stand.

Behind much of the hostility over revolutionary strategy was the historical distrust between the Russians and the Chinese. In the 1970's, even after China had softened its revolutionary line, it still went on denouncing the Soviet Union.

By far the most explosive issue in the Sino-Soviet dispute was their quarrel over border territories. This involves some 350,000 square miles.

The Chinese claim that the disputed lands were taken from China by the Russian czars in the 19th century. At that time China's Manchu rulers were too feeble to resist foreign demands and were forced to accept "unequal treaties."

☆ ☆ ☆ ☆ ☆ ☆ ☆ ☆ ☆ ☆

Relations between the U.S. and the People's Republic of China, chilly from the start, became bitterly angry during the Korean War. In the shock of China's unexpected entrance into the Korean fighting, American attitudes hardened. In 1954 the U.S. and the Nationalist Chinese signed a mutual security treaty, opening the way to massive U.S. military and economic aid to Taiwan.

The U.S. government continued to back the Chinese Nationalist regime in its claim to being the legitimate government of all of China. The U.S. refused to recognize the People's Republic and fought to keep it out of the United Nations.

Nor was China exactly pleased with the U.S. Throughout the 1950's and 1960's, the U.S. was villain number one in China. "Hate America" campaigns became a standard feature of Chinese Communist life.

Then, around 1970, the hostility between the two sides seemed to ease. Both sides began to rethink their positions. Why did this happen? No doubt there were many different reasons, but the following probably played the most important part:

1. China, emerging from the chaos of the Cultural Revolution, began to look outward to friendlier relations with foreign lands.

2. Fearing the Soviet Union, Chinese leaders sought to better relations with the United States. This, they hoped, might prevent the U.S. and the Soviet Union from forming an alliance against China.

Teng Hsiao-ping visited the Johnson Space Center in Houston, Texas, in 1979 to demonstrate his determination to modernize China.

3. In the U.S., the belief grew that while China often "talked tough," it often did not act as aggressively as it talked.

4. The U.S. recognized that the world's most populous nation was fast becoming a superpower.

The thaw in U.S.-China relations showed its first effects in the United Nations. Since the founding of the U.N. at the end of World War II, Nationalist China had held the China seat in the U.N., including a permanent seat on the Security Council. The U.S. consistently opposed a resolution to seat Communist China and to expel Nationalist China. Then, in 1971, the U.S. changed its vote. The People's Republic took the China seat in the U.N., and the Nationalists were expelled.

A few months later, there was another stunning event. President Richard M. Nixon flew to China for a week-long visit which Nixon called the "week that changed the world." It was the first meeting ever between leaders of the two governments. They agreed to work toward closer ties in the future.

Change came slowly, in part because both countries had problems at home to worry about. In the U.S., the Watergate scandal exploded, and President Nixon resigned. In China, a struggle between radicals and moderates came to the boiling point when Mao died.

Finally, in the winter of 1978-79, the thaw became official. President Jimmy Carter announced that the U.S. would cut off its formal ties with Taiwan and give full recognition to the Peking government. Early in 1979, Deputy Premier Teng Hsiao-ping visited the U.S. to discuss trade and other contacts between the two countries. As he left, he said: "We came with a message of friendship from the Chinese people to the American people."

This official change did not, of course, mean that problems and conflicts were over. Some Americans were unhappy with the change, especially with what they saw as the "abandonment" of Taiwan. In China, officials worried that Western visitors and goods were spreading too many Western ideas.

The U.S. and China remained far apart in their systems of government and in their outlooks on the world. But the extreme fear and hostility of the 1950's and 1960's had gone and seemed unlikely to return.

Double-check

Review

1. Briefly summarize China's relations with the United States and the Soviet Union in the 1950's, 1960's, 1970's, and 1980's.

2. What reason did the Chinese give for their 1979 invasion of Vietnam?

3. What has been the most explosive issue in the Chinese quarrels with the Soviet Union?

4. What did Chinese leadership hope to prevent by seeking better relations with the United States?

5. Who was the Chinese government official who visited the United States in early 1979?

Discussion

1. How does Chinese communism differ from Soviet communism? How is it similar? What aspects of Chinese culture may cause the differences?

2. How large a role do you think China's centuries of "humiliation" will play in China's domestic and foreign policies in the future? Give reasons for your answer.

3. As this chapter points out, during the 1950's and 1960's, the U.S. was "villain number one" in China. At the same time, many U.S. politicians spoke about "evil Communists" and a "Red Menace." Can such feelings be overcome? If not, why not? If so, how can it be done?

Activities

1. Two students might role-play the first meeting of a Chinese and a U.S. diplomat in the early 1970's. Each should try to explain the reasons for their government's statements and actions during the 1950's and 1960's, and then present reasons why the two nations should trust each other and cooperate in the future. Afterward, the rest of the class could pretend to be reporters asking the diplomats questions about their statements and future plans.

2. A committee of students might watch TV, newspapers, and magazines for reports on developments between the U.S. and China. Articles and photos could be displayed on a bulletin board under appropriate headings.

3. Some students might research and report to the class on China's 20th-century relationships with its neighbors. Possible topics might include: The Korean War; Chinese-Soviet Border Disputes; China's Invasion of Vietnam; China's Trade Agreements with Japan.

THREE NATIONS

	P.R.C.	U.S.	U.S.S.R.
Population* (mid-1984 est.)	1,034,500,000	236,300,000	247,000,000
Population under age 15 (percent)*	34%	22%	25%
Population over 64 (percent)*	5%	12%	10%
Urban population	21%	74%	64.8%
Population projection in year 2000*	1,303,700,000	268,000,000	316,000,000
Area (sq. miles)**	3,691,502	3,615,122	8,467,250
Population density (per sq. mi.)**	349.8	65	31.6
Armed Forces*** Regular	159,299,000	2,022,000	55,070,000
Reserves	126,214,000	797,000	10,391,000

Sources: Population Reference Bureau
**ABC-Clio Kaleidoscope Data
***CIA World Factbook

Use the table above and information in Chapter 21 to answer the following questions.

1. What is the source of most of the population statistics in this table? What do P.R.C., U.S. and U.S.S.R. stand for?

2. How do these nations rank according to population? According to size?

3. In which categories does China rank first?

4. Which nation might be called the "least crowded"? Why?

5. Which statistic might possibly be a factor in certain disputes between China and the U.S.S.R.?

THE ABC'S OF CHANGE

THERE IS A TV in the meeting room of the Peking factory where Chung works. (You met Chung in Chapter 17.) He likes to watch programs showing the different kinds of lives that people lead throughout the country.

Each program begins with a title card that tells which television studio produced it. The studio's name is written in Chinese characters, of course. But underneath, in the letters of the Western alphabet, the title card also says "Beijing Dianshitai," meaning "Peking Television."

For many years the Chinese government has been pushing the use of the alphabet along with characters. On official posters, street signs, and other public notices, all or part of the message is repeated in Roman letters.

There are practical reasons for this. It takes a long time to learn to use the traditional characters. Each character has to be memorized by itself. But once a person knows the sounds of each letter in the alphabet, he or she can read and write any word. If China switched entirely to the alphabet, its school children could learn to handle the language much more quickly.

Even for people who know the characters, using them can be time-consuming. The most modern Chinese typewriter is a huge, slow-moving machine. And it contains only the 2,000 most common characters, at that.

Switching to the alphabet may have useful side effects. A Chinese author who lived earlier in this century wrote a famous article called "Silent China." In it, he blamed the language, and especially the writing system, for the fact that other nations took little notice of China. The Chinese could talk and write all they wanted, he said, but their language was too different for it to get across to other peoples. China might just as well be silent.

Today the Chinese government wants the rest of the world to hear it. Using the Western alphabet could make communication, both ways, just a little bit easier.

For Americans, however, there is one slight problem.

The way the Chinese spell their words is not the same as the system that became common in the U.S.

For example, the name of China's former leader has traditionally been spelled Mao Tse-tung in the U.S. In the Chinese system, it's Mao Zedong.

The vowels in the new system have not changed much. As in the old system, each vowel is pronounced separately. In the "Bei" of *Beijing,* for example, you combine the "e" of *bet* with the "i" of *hit*. The result sounds very much like the English word *bay*.

Most of the consonants have their usual English sounds. But there are two ringers. The "q" stands for a *ch* sound and the "x," for a *sh*. These are in addition to sounds that are spelled "ch" and "sh." They are close enough that you can pronounce "q" the same as *ch* and "x" the same as *sh*.

The Chinese spelling system is called *pinyin,* which means "phonetic spelling." Compared to the English system, it gives a closer idea of the actual Chinese sounds. When Chung pronounces the name of his hometown, it sounds much more like "Beijing" than "Peking."

Throughout this book we have used the familiar English spellings. However, the Spelling and Pronunciation Guide on pages 230-234 lists the *pinyin* spelling of all key words and names. Since the beginning of 1979, the U.S. government has officially adopted the *pinyin* system. Most U.S. newspapers and magazines now use it too.

Despite its advantages, *pinyin* does pose one problem for the Chinese. As we saw in Chapter 5, there are several different Chinese languages. All use the same characters for the same words, but pronounce them very differently. *Pinyin* gives only the pronunciation of Mandarin, the majority language. For Chinese who speak the languages of Canton or Shanghai, *pinyin* does not come naturally.

Still, over the centuries, the Chinese have struggled through wars, rebellions, earthquakes, floods, and backbreaking labor. The problems of *pinyin* are unlikely to defeat them.

EPILOGUE

THE ONGOING REVOLUTION

THE 20TH CENTURY has seen mainland China move rapidly from a troubled, weak society to a powerful Communist state. It has also seen this Communist state go through some startling shifts in policy. What has really changed in China? What has remained the same?

Despite the changes in labels, the basic structure of Chinese society has remained authoritarian in form. In other words, China has always stressed obedience to authority over individual needs and still does today. Democracy as it is understood in the West has not been able to take root in China's soil.

Within this overall picture, however, great changes have taken place in the Chinese People's Republic. The traditional authority of Confucianism has been replaced by the authority of communism. First loyalty has shifted from the family to the nation.

There has also been a leveling of Chinese society. The yawning gap between the few who had much and the many who had little has been, if not eliminated, very much narrowed. Consider also the changed role of women in China. In old China, men ordered, women obeyed. Today, according to a visiting Indian social scientist, "The Chinese woman has become the equal of men . . . legally, politically, and morally."

Many of China's age-old problems remain. There is still the problem of limited farmland to support a huge population. And the job of converting an agricultural society into a modern industrial state is overwhelming. This is especially so under conditions in which two thirds of the population must till the soil endlessly to meet the basic needs of life. In China there is little surplus to plow into industrial development.

In some ways, to be sure, the Chinese People's Republic has made impressive industrial gains. China is now capable of producing without foreign help much of its own heavy equipment: trucks, tractors, machine tools, ships. It has exploded hydrogen bombs and sent space satellites into orbit.

But mainland China's industrial output becomes a

lot less impressive when its enormous population is taken into account. Living standards in China will be a long time in catching up to those in the industrially developed nations — if they ever do.

Whatever the obstacles, though, China is clearly determined to have an important role in the world. Mao's successors had this future importance in mind when they gave top priority to economic growth.

What role will China play on the world stage of the future? It is possible that the pendulum might swing back to revolutionary fervor, and that China might once again turn its back on the rest of the world. Even so, it seems unlikely that the nation would seethe with quite as much fury as it did in the 1960's.

After all, it was Mao, not a young radical, who had triggered the Cultural Revolution. In a sense, he wanted to turn back the clock, to make China relive the excitement of the past. The central struggle of the Cultural Revolution was not between young Red Guards and not-so-young officials. It was among the old-timers of the Communist Party.

Today the surviving oldtimers are in their seventies and eighties. Soon the government of China will fall into the hands of people who took no part in the struggles before 1949. They will probably have little interest in reviving the past.

If China's future leaders do follow the practical course of the 1970's, the results may still be revolutionary. China's sheer numbers place it in a class by itself. Some experts believe that the population has already passed the one billion mark and may hit 1¼ billion by the year 2000. A nation consisting of one fourth of earth's humanity, growing in strength and prosperity, is bound to become a new and important force in the world. The fate of China's millions will have an impact on the future of us all.

Spelling and Pronunciation Guide

In this guide, Chinese names are listed under their old spellings. For names in current use, the new spellings are given in parentheses ( ) immediately afterward. In a few cases, the two spellings are the same.

The pronunciation of each word follows the dash (—). Well-known names such as *Peking* and *Hong Kong* have acquired "English" pronunciations of their own. In such cases, the English version is given first, followed by the Chinese pronunciation in parentheses.

The new spelling system, known as *pinyin,* gives a more accurate idea of Chinese pronunciation. All of the letters except two are pronounced normally. The "q" is a soft *ch* sound, and the "x" stands for a soft *sh*. (See pages 222-223 for more on *pinyin.*)

There are no accented syllables in Chinese as there are in English. However, some of the most common names are pronounced in English with accented syllables, and these are shown in the guide. Syllables set in capitals are accented.

The following system translates each sound into the nearest common English equivalent.

230

a (as in cat)
ah (as in odd)
aw (as in lawn)
ay (as in ale)
ch (as in chair)
e (as in silent)
ee (as in eat)
eh (as in end)
ew (as in few)
g (as in go)
i (as in charity)
ie (as in ice)
ih (as in ill)
j (as in John)
k (as in keep)

o (as in connect)
oh (as in old)
oo (as in too)
or (as in for)
ow (as in out)
oy (as in boy)
s (as in sit)
sh (as in ship)
t (as in tin)
th (as in then)
u (as in circus)
uh (unaccented a as in soft)
ur (as in urn)
y (as in yet)
z (as in zebra)

Amur River (Heilongjiang) — uh-MOOR (hay-loong-jahng)
Analects — AN-uh-lekts
Anhwei (Anhui)— ahn-wee

Buddha — BOO-dah

calligraphy — kuh-LIG-ruh-fee
Canton (Guangdong province, Guangzhou city) — kan-TAHN
(gwahng-doong, gwahng-zhoh)
Chang-ch'un (Changchun) — chahng-choon
Chekiang (Zhijiang) — juh-jahng
Chengchow (Zhengzhou) — juhng-jow
Cheng-tu (Chengdu) — chung-doo
chi — chee
Chiang Ching (Jiang Qing) — jahng ching
Chiang Kai-shek — JAHNG kie-SHEHK
Ch'in — chin
Ch'ing — ching
Chou — joh
Chou En-lai (Zhou Enlai) — JOH en-LIE
Ch'u Yuan — choo yoo-an
Chu Yuan-chang — joo yoo-an-jahng
Ch'uan-chou (Quanzhou) — choo-an-jow

Chuang — juahng
Chung — joong
Chungking (Chongqing) — choong-king (choong-ching)
Chung-kuo (Zhongguo) — joong-gwoh
Chung-kuo jen (Zhongguo ren) — joong-gwoh run
Confucius — kahn-FEW-shus

Fu-chou (Fuzhou) — foo-joh
Fukien (Fujian) — foo-jahn
Fushan (Fushun) — foo-shun

Siddhartha Gautama — sih-DAHR-tuh GOH-tuh-muh
Genghis Khan — JEHNG-gihs KAHN
Greater Khingan Range (Daxing Anlingshan) — king-an
   (dah-shing an-ling-shan)
Gum San — gum sahn

Haerbin (Harbin) — hahr-bin
Han — hahn
Hankow (Hangzhou) — hahng-joh
Heilungkiang (Heilongjiang) — hay-loong-jahng
Honan (Honan) — hoh-nahn
Hong Kong (Xianggang) — HAHNG kahng (shahng-gahng)
Hopeh (Hebei) — hoh-bay
Hsi Kiang (Xijiang) — shee jahng
Hsiang — shee-ahng
hua-chiao — hoo-ah-jow
Hua Kuo-feng (Hua Guofeng) — hoo-ah gwoh-feng
Hunan (Hunan) — hoo-nahn
Hupeh (Hubei) — hoo-bay
Hwang Ho (Huanghe) — hoo-ahng huh

Ilha Formosa — EEL-yuh for-MOH-suh
Inner Mongolian Autonomous Republic (Nei Monggol) —
   mahn-GOH-lee-un aw-TAH-nuh-mus (nay moong-gool)

kang — kung
Kansu (Gansu) — gahn-soo
Kiangsi (Jiangxi) — jahng-shee
Kiangsu (Jiangsu) — jahng-soo
Kirin (Jilin) — juh-lin
Kuala Lumpur — koo-AH-luh LOOM-poor
Kublai Khan — KOOB-lie KAHN

Kung Fu-tzu — goong foo-dzuh
Kunlun Mountains (Kunlunshan) — koon-loon (shahn)
Kunming (Kunming) — koon-ming
Kuomintang (Guomindang) — gwoh-ming-dahng
Kwangsi Autonomous Republic (Guangxi Zhuang) —
  gwahng-shee aw-TAH-nuh-mus (joo-ahng)
Kweichow (Guizhou) — gwee-joh

Lao-tzu — low-dzuh
Lhasa (Lhasa) — LAH-sah
Li T'ai-po — lee tie-boh
Liaoning (Liaoning) — lee-ow-ning
Lu — loo
Lu-ta (Luda) — loo-dah

Macao — muh-COW
Manchu — MAHN-joo
Mandarin — MAN-duh-rin
Mao Tse-tung (Mao Zedong) — MOW dzuh-DOONG
Mencius — men-shus
Meng-tzu — mung-dzuh
Ming — ming
Mongol — MAHNG-guhl
mou — moh

Nan-ching (Nanjing) — nahn-jing
Ningsia Autonomous Republic (Ningxia Hui) — ning-shah
  aw-TAH-nuh-mus (hoo-ee)
Nirvana — nur-VAH-nuh

P'an-ku — pahn-koo
Peking (Beijing) — pee-KING (bay-jing)
pinyin — peen-yeen
Pythagoras — puh-THAG-uh-rus

queue — kew

Shang — shahng
Shanghai (Shanghai) — shahng-hie
Shang-tu (Chengde) — chung-duh
Shansi (Shanxi) — shahn-shee
Shantung (Shandong) — shahn-doong
Shensi (Shaanxi) — shahn-see

Shenyang (Shenyang) — shun-yahng
Shih Huang-ti — shee hoo-ahng-tee
Sian (Xian) — shee-ahn
Sinkiang Uigur Autonomous Republic (Xinjiang Uygur) —
    sheen-jahng wee-goor aw-TAH-nuh-mus
Sun Yat-sen — soon yaht-sehn
Sung — soong
Szechwan (Sichuan) — seech-wahn

Taipei — tie-PAY
Taiwan — tie-WAHN
Takla Makan Desert (Talimupendi) — TAHK-luh MAH-kun
    (tah-lee-moo-pehn-dee)
T'ang — tahng
Tao — dow
Taoism — DOW-iz-um
Temujin — DEH-moo-jeen
Teng Fu-lai (Deng Fulai) — duhng foo-lie
Teng Hsiao-ping (Deng Xiaoping) — duhng show-ping
Tibetan Autonomous Republic (Xizang) — tih-BEH-tun
    aw-TAH-nuh-mus (shee-zahng)
Tien Shan Mountains (Tianshan) — tee-ahn shahn
Tientsin (Tianjin) — tee-ahn-jeen
Tsinghai (Qinghai) — ching-hie
Tsingtao (Qingdao) — ching-dow
Tzu Hsi — zoo shee

Uigurs — WEE-gorz

Wang Hsi-chih (Wang Xiji) — wahng shee-jee
Wang Ying-li (Wang Yingli) — wahng ying-lee
Wang Ying-ling (Wang Yingling) — wahng ying-ling
Wang Ying-ma (Wang Yingma) — wahng ying-mah
Wu-han (Wuhan) — woo-hahn
Wu I Mountains (Wuyishan) — woo yee (shahn)

Yalung (Yalong) — yah-loong
Yangtze Kiang (Yangzijiang) — yahng-zee kee-ahng
    (yahng-dzee-jahng)
Yenan (Yanan) — yah-nahn
Yuan Shih-kai — yoo-ahng shee-kie
Yunnan (Yunnan) — yoon-nahn

Index

---

*Photograph

235

CAL WORKS OF AMY LOWELL, Houghton Mifflin Company • 67, Pictorial Parade • 69, G. Damian Loescher from Pictorial Parade • 71, Courtesy of the Smithsonian Institution, Freer Gallery of Art, Washington, D.C. • 76, The Metropolitan Museum of Art, Gift of Heber R. Bishop, 1902 • 81, KENG CHIH T'U • 84-85, The Metropolitan Museum of Art, Fletcher Fund, 1947. The A.W. Bahr Collection • 90, Inger McCabe from Rapho Guillumette • 92, 94, Marc Riboud/MAGNUM • 97, René Burri/MAGNUM • 103, Tokyo National University of Fine Arts and Music • 107, Bibliothèque Nationale, Paris • 112, René Burri/MAGNUM • 113, Eastfoto • 114, (top) Roland and Sabrina Michaud from Rapho Guillumette; (bottom) Eastfoto • 115 (top, bottom), Eastfoto • 118, 119 (top, bottom), 120, Eastfoto • 121, Henri Cartier-Bresson/MAGNUM • 122, Eastfoto • 123, (top) UPI; (bottom) Eastfoto • 124, (top) Henri Cartier-Bresson/MAGNUM; (bottom) Caio Mario Garrubba from Rapho Guillumette • 125, G. Damian Loescher from Pictorial Parade • 126, Government of the Republic of China • 127, Courtesy, Museum of Fine Arts, Boston. Fund, Ross Collection • 128, (top left) Courtesy of the Fogg Art Museum, Harvard University. Bequest, Grenville L. Winthrop; (bottom right) GREEN DRAGON VASE, Chinese K'ang-hsi Period, National Gallery of Art, Widener Collection • 129, (top) Marc Riboud/MAGNUM; (bottom) The Metropolitan Museum of Art, The A.W. Bahr Collection, 1947 • 130, Brian Brake from Rapho Guillumette • 131, (top) G. Damian Loescher from Pictorial Parade; (bottom) Marc Riboud/MAGNUM • 132, Henri Cartier-Bresson/MAGNUM • 135, Berry-Hill Galleries, Inc., New York • 139, London Daily Express from Pictorial Parade • 144, 146, UPI • 152, Paul Guillumette from Rapho Guillumette • 154, UPI • 162, 164, Eastfoto • 167, Henri Cartier-Bresson/MAGNUM • 172, Caio Mario Garrubba from Rapho Guillumette • 175, (top) UPI; (bottom) H. Bureau/Sygma • 177,178, UPI • 180, Nik Wheeler from Black Star • 181, Wally McNamee from Woodfin Camp and Associates • 184, Caio Mario Garrubba from Rapho Guillumette • 188, Marc Riboud/MAGNUM • 190, René Burri/MAGNUM • 191, Henri Cartier-Bresson/MAGNUM • 197, UPI • 204, Southern Pacific • 206, Georg Gerster from Rapho Guillumette • 208, Brian Brake from Rapho Guillumette • 210, Rocky Weldon from Leo deWys, Inc. • 216, 217, 218, Sygma • 221, NASA • 227, Marc Riboud/MAGNUM • COVER, Nancy Henningsen. MAPS by Irmgard Lochner, Wilhelmina Reyinga.